Bruno Santi

Raphael

Scala Books
Distributed by Harper & Row, Publishers

© 1977 by Scala, Istituto Fotografico Editoriale, Firenze

Design: Scala

Translation: Paul Blanchard

Photographs: Scala, except on pages 6, 17, 23, 37 (National Gallery, London); 14 (Photo Braun, Mulhouse); 14, 19, 36, 55 (National Gallery, Washington); 16 (Photo Giraudon, Paris); 18 (Réunion des Musées Nationaux, Paris); 26 (Kunsthistorisches Museum, Wien); 72 (Victoria and Albert Museum, London)

Produced by Scala, Istituto Fotografico Editoriale

Printed in Italy in 1981
by Officine Grafiche Firenze

The Life and Art of Raphael

The Environment of Umbria and Urbino

Raphael Sanzio was born in Urbino on April 6, 1483, a year after the death of Duke Frederick II. As Urbino's political leader and major artistic patron, Frederick had transformed the small hill town near the borders of Romagna, Tuscany and the Marche into a prosperous city which gathered cultural influences from the north and center of the Italian peninsula and which occupied an advanced position in the fields of art, literature and courtly custom in the last decades of the Quattrocento.

Urbino's good fortune grew with Frederick and outlived him by very little, for Urbino was surrounded by powerful neighbors: Venice, Florence and the Papal States. The Duke had unified the Duchy of Montefeltro, which was legally under Papal power but which had actually split into many small feudal possessions. As the organizer of mercenary armies which he placed at the disposal of various Italian states, he increased his personal treasure and contributed greatly to the wealth of his city, which in this way came to know the most prosperous moment in its history.

This prosperity permitted numerous cultural and artistic initiatives, many of which are still visible today. Artists like Paolo Uccello—whose *Miracle of the Host* (1465-1469) is one of the freshest and liveliest narratives of the Quattrocento—and Piero della Francesca—who executed several masterpieces, among them the *Flagellation* (1455) and the *Portraits* of Duke Frederick and Battista Sforza, his wife (1465)—were attracted by the generosity of the leader-patron and by the initiatives and projects he proposed. Afterwards came those who showed themselves to be closest to the personality of the Duke, in thought and deed: Justus of Ghent (who, in Urbino, combined the analytical characteristics of Flemish painting and the values of light and synthesis established by Piero della Francesca), Melozzo da Forlì, Filippo Brunelleschi, Luciano and Francesco Laurana, Francesco di Giorgio Martini (sculptor, painter and builder of fortifications) and Giorgio Schiavone.

This mixture of presences and activities gave rise to the construction of the massive and fanciful Ducal Palace and to the creation of a vast and notable artistic circle.

Urbino was capable of mediating the most varied artistic tendencies, from the Venetian to the Florentine to the Umbrian. Its culturally and artistically fertile ground formed the substratum in which the composite and receptive art of Raphael is rooted.

Raphael was born, as we said, on April 6, 1483, to Giovanni Santi and Màgia Ciarla. His father, a painter, was well known in artistic circles in Urbino, even if he is better known in the history of art for his poetic eulogy of contemporary painting contained in the *Chronicle* of the deeds of Frederick II, written immediately after the Duke's death. His works contain motifs from various sources, among them Piero, Perugino (active in the Marche in Fano and Senigallia, minor towns in the Duchy of Montefeltro) and Melozzo da Forlì.

Two artists were working in his father's workshop during Raffael's childhood. Evangelista da Pian di Meleto (whose artistic production has yet to be reconstructed) and Timoteo Viti da Urbino, who returned to his native Urbino from Bologna in 1495. The latter undoubtedly more deeply influenced the very young Raphael. The elements which this painter lacks—a sense of proportion and of composition—are visible in Raphael's early works, the first of which is, in Longhi's opinion, the *Banner* of Città di Castello (c. 1499). This work, which is in effect two paintings placed back to back, represents the *Crucifixion* on one side and the *Madonna of Mercy* on the other. The masterfully executed Madonna reflects the art of Piero della Francesca.

Around the beginning of the 16th century Raphael met Pietro Perugino (c. 1455-1523), who influenced his painting perhaps more than any other painter. Perugino, who had been praised by Raphael's father in the *Chronicle*, reached his greatest fame in the last years of the Quattrocento. In addition, documents show that Raphael collaborated with Evangelista di Pian di Meleto on the altarpiece commissioned in 1510 for the church of Sant'Agostino in Città di Castello. This piece, whose surviving parts are now dispersed in various European and American museums, shows Peruginesque motifs, identifiable in the poses and features of the figures, though the grace of the compositions and the firmness of the figures surpass Perugino's capabilities.

As Venturi affirms, there must have been a « thorough familiarity with the master » behind « such a [profound] absorption of Peruginesque elements » in this early work by Raphael. Perhaps the only opportunity the young painter had to assist the master was provided by a fresco for the Collegio del Cambio in Perugia (1500). Here some critics, supported by tradition, claim to see the hand of the nineteen year old Raphael in the figure of *Fortitude*, which recalls certain aspects of Francesco Francia as trasmitted by Timoteo Viti, his close follower.

Perugino's fresco for the Collegio del Cambio is followed chronologically by the *Resurrection* of 1501 in the Vatican Museum. This painting has also been cited as a work of collaboration by critics anxious to reconstruct the activity of the young Raphael during his association with Perugino. But today most critics agree that nothing in this panel—which is characteristic of the weak and mannered art which Perugino produced during this period—reveals Raphael's hand.

The contrary is true for the *St. Sebastian* in the Carrara Academy in Bergamo. Here graceful Peruginesque poses and the hazy transparency of color characteristic of Francesco Francia are fused together in a way which clearly indicates Raphael's presence. His ability to compose clear and balanced forms becomes typical from this work on, as does the discreet and harmonious distillation of the formal elements of other painters in the clear, serene vision which seems characteristic of his artistic temperament.

If the *St. Sebastian* can truly be attributed to this period in Raphael's development, saturated as it is in Umbrian culture and nurtured on Peruginesque references, it seems impossible to attribute to him the *Portrait of a Youth*—also of high quality—in the Uffizi. A certain uneasiness in the youth's physiognomy and the accentuated chiaroscuro seem to exclude the possibility that Raphael painted this portrait. It seems instead to be a Florentine work, possibily from the workshop of Leonardo. Nevertheless, the tendency expressed by some critics to attribute it to Lorenzo di Credi, pupil of Verrocchio and interpreter of Leonardo's first style, seems hazardous.

The presence of Peruginesque motifs in Raphael's work is still quite evident in the *Crucifixion* of 1502-1503, now in the National Gallery in London. This painting originally formed the central part of an altarpiece commissioned for the church of San Domenico in Città di Castello. It is the first work that Raphael signed. The signature, "Painted by Raphael of Urbino," documents his full artistic autonomy and indicates his background.

The composition derives from other panels on the same subject painted by Perugino; for example, the imposing Chigi altarpiece for Sant'Agostino in Siena. But the rigorous correspondences of gesture which decisively distinguish Raphael's figures from the sentimental and obvious poses of the master, clearly set the young pupil apart. The faces are treated with a subtler chiaroscuro and the volumes are, as a result, more slender than those of Perugino. Thus Raphael—even though he is unwilling and, perhaps, unable to break away from Perugino's influence—shows his true temperament in this painting. This temperament includes an extraordinary feeling for proportion and an acute visual sensibility. It is even more evident in the two predella compartments—one in the Cook collection in Richmond and the other in the Lisbon Gallery— with stories from the life of St. Jerome.

The works which conclude the young painter's Umbrian

Opposite page, above: School of Perugino,
Portrait of Perugino. Florence, Uffizi.
This painting has been attributed to various
sources. It was finally identified as a portrait
of Raphael's master in 1935. The features correspond
to those of the self-portrait that Perugino painted
in the Collegio del Cambio, in Perugia.

Opposite page, below: School of Perugino,
Resurrection. Rome, Vatican Museum.
Nineteenth century critics claimed to see Raphael's
hand in this panel, which was executed after
the Cambio frescoes. Modern critics deny that Raphael
participated in its execution. The painting
is dated 1501 and is referred
to the late activity of the Umbrian master.

Left: St. Sebastian. Bergamo, Accademia Carrara.
This panel, whose origins are unknown, has been
widely recognized as one of Raphael's first
autonomous works. It is dated 1501-02.

Right: 16th century Florentine School,
Portrait of a Youth. Florence, Uffizi.
The portrait, attributed to Lorenzo di Credi
and then to Raphael, is probably the work of an early
16th century Florentine painter influenced by Leonardo.

*Crucifixion with Saints Mary,
John, Jerome and Mary Magdalen
(Città di Castello Altarpiece).
London, National Gallery.
This is Raphael's first signed work.
It was painted in 1502-1503
for the church of San Domenico
in Città di Castello, where
Raphael worked for several
patrons during the first years
of the 16th century.*

apprenticeship date to the years immediately after the London *Crucifixion*. They represent steps in a slow process which leads from the rejection of assimilated forms to a search for new figurative elements through which the artist can express his needs for clarity and formal balance.

In 1502-1503 Raphael also executed the *Coronation of the Virgin*, now in the Vatican Museum. This commission, originally intended for the church of San Francesco al Monte in Perugia, was first awarded to Perugino, who entrusted it to his pupil. The altarpiece combines two scenes common in Quattrocento iconography: the *Coronation* (which occupies the upper part of the picture space) and *The Giving of the Girdle to St. Thomas* (in the lower part), an episode traditionally associated with the Assumption. The two scenes remain separate from one another, and this clear division of the composition may indicate the painter's uncertainty of his compositional abilities. Nevertheless, the forms are already mature and

*Coronation of the Virgin
(Oddi Altarpiece).
Rome, Vatican Museum.
The panel, commissioned to
the artist in 1502 by Maddalena
degli Oddi for the church
of San Francesco in Perugia,
combines the two traditional
representations of the Coronation
and Assumption of the Virgin
in a single harmonic composition.*

certain perspective innovations—such as the diagonal re-presentation of the Madonna's tomb—constitute a departure from traditional Quattrocento compositional types. Extant drawings demonstrate the tremendous amount of thought which Raphael put into the panel's realization and some details, notably the highly individuated faces of the Apostles and the serene landscape in the background, are quite masterful. But the most meaningful passages are found in the predella scenes: the vast space which opens up beneath the colonnades of the *Annunciation;* the highly animated *Adoration of the Magi;* and the free quality of the atmosphere in the *Presentation in the Temple,* which foreshadows the extraordinary spatial intuition of some of the artist's future Vatican compositions.

Raphael is ready for new figurative experiments after these accomplishments. The necessity for finding further elements to add to traditional modes of representation leads him to Florence. Here a great demand for artists of all backgrounds continued to thrive, notwithstanding the terrible upheaval which the city suffered during this period.

Florence at the turn of the century was in the midst of a vast cultural and political crisis. Many of the artists who had developed the cultural values which characterized the city during the Quattrocento had either died or gone elsewhere and, as a result, these values were beginning to lose their splendor. This cultural crisis was complicated by political events, such as the invasion of Charles VIII of France and the consequent expulsion of Piero di Lorenzo de' Medici in 1494, and the dramatic experience of Savonarola which culminated in the public burning of the friar in 1498. Nevertheless, a great demand for artists of all backgrounds continued to exist. Many important works of art had survived the city's spiritual and political trauma and public participation in the artistic process was, as always, more lively in Florence than elsewhere.

One must not interpret Raphael's Florentine experience as a prolonged stay, for it was at most a series of brief visits which permitted him to come into contact with some of the artists present there. The numerous works which Umbrian commissions continued to draw from him suggest that Raphael returned to Perugia frequently.

One such work is the celebrated *Marriage of the Virgin (Lo sposalizio)* now in the Brera Museum in Milan. This panel was commissioned by the Albizzini family of Città di Castello and was destined for the church of San Francesco. Critics believe the painting to be inspired by two compositions by Perugino: the celebrated *Giving of the Keys* from the fresco cycle in the Sistine Chapel and a panel containing the *Marriage of the Virgin* presently in the Museum of Caen. The structure of Raphael's painting, which includes figures in the foreground and a centralized building in the background, can certainly be compared to the two Perugino paintings. But Raphael's painting features a well developed circular composition, while that of Perugino is developed horizontally, in a way still characteristic of the Quattrocento. The construction of the figure group and of the large polygonal building clearly distinguish Raphael's painting from that of his master. The space is more open in Raphael's composition, indicating a command of perspective which is superior to Perugino's. Some critics believe that Raphael's perspective construction reflects the architectonic research of Leonardo da Vinci and Donato Bramante. The work, signed and dated 1504, provides a clear indication of Raphael's style during this period.

Another Umbrian commission which seems to be bound up with Raphael's first visit to Florence and which presupposes, as we have noted, that the artist returned to Perugia, is the *Colonna Altarpiece* in the Metropolitan Museum, New York. The work is also called the *Madonna Enthroned with Saints Peter, Catherine of Alexandria, John, Cecilia (or Margaret) and Paul*. It was executed for the Sisters of St. Anthony of Perugia and it is generally dated 1503-1505. Figurative elements which echo the style of Perugino and traces of Florentine painting from the first years of the Cinquecento, appear here in equal measure. The compositional structure of the angels in the lunette still typifies the Umbrian tradition, but a soft chiaroscuro which may derive from Leonardo is visible in the face of the central figure of God the Father. The vigorously conceived saints of the altarpiece itself recall the technique of Fra Bartolomeo della Porta, the Florentine painter and Dominican friar whose influence on Raphael's style is explained in greater detail below. This is particularly true for the figure of St. Paul, constructed in the decisively monumental way which typifies the friar's style.

The three predella panels, containing representations of *The Way to Calvary*, the *Agony in the Garden* and the *Pietà*, surpass the figurative themes of the preceding century. In all three panels the atmospheric effects are freer than in previous works and the figures are more autonomous in the space they occupy. The sculptural quality of the *Way to Calvary* represents a definite departure from Quattrocento decorative tendencies. Raphael's encounter with contemporary Florentine art has begun to push the teachings of Perugino into the background and to prepare the way for the complete autonomy of expression which reveals itself in the following year.

Raphael in Florence

In 1505 Raphael is in Florence. The most notable artists active at the time are Leonardo da Vinci (born in 1452), Michelangelo Buonarroti (born in 1475) and the above-mentioned Dominican friar, Bartolommeo della Porta (born in or around 1472). Each of these artists had developed a different style of painting, but all were involved in a search for figurative elements which surpassed the Quattrocento models and for an expressive language in which color was more unified and space was freer.

Raphael became decisively involved in this search, which goes beyond the lively curiosity of the first Florentine Renaissance and presupposes a new breadth of forms and a greater freedom of thought. Leonardesque "shading," which fused the representation of man and nature together in a single vision, replaced the Quattrocento notion of "functional line" (to use Berenson's term), the clearly defined contour which both delineated the figure and represented its movement. At the same time, a new, more monumental compositional type arose (though essentially new, it had already been foreshadowed in the works of some Quattrocento masters, for example, in the *San Barnaba Altarpiece* by Botticelli, 1486). It first appears in the art of Fra Bartolommeo who, for the moment, seems to be the artist to whom Raphael turns most of his attention.

Raphael abandons every trace of Peruginesque influence in Florence and returns to Umbria in the same year with new pictorial motifs which he will express in two notable works, the *Colonna Altarpiece* (which we have already examined) and, a bit later, the *Ansidei Madonna*, also known as the *Enthroned Madonna with Saints John the Baptist and Nicholas of Bari*. This *Sacra Conversazione*, attributed to the years 1505-1506, shows the Virgin attentively reading a prayer book, with the Child in her lap. The two saints stand at her sides. The Baptist points to the Child (a traditional iconographic device) and St. Nicholas is absorbed in a volume which he holds in his hand. The luminous landscape background and the high baldachin remotely recall the art of Piero della Francesca, but the figure types, still vaguely Peruginesque in their contours, are psychologically more complex and structurally more volumetric. The compositional scheme is reduced to a large arch whose central axis is represented by the baldachin. The result is a sense of monu-

*Annunciation,
Adoration of the Magi,
and Presentation
at the Temple. Rome,
Vatican Museum.
These three episodes
are part of the
predella of the
Oddi Alterpiece.
They clearly
demonstrate the
sense of composition
and the broad,
comprehensive
vision that typify
Raphael's paintings.*

mentality and harmonic proportion which we will find constant in Raphael's art.

The figurative powers which Raphael developed in Florence led to "a more synthetic conception of form, a refinement of intellectual expression" (Venturi), which are visible in the *Knight's Dream* in the National Gallery, London, and the *Three Graces* of Chantilly. Critics believe that the two panels may have formed a single diptych presented to Scipione di Tommaso Borghese at his birth, in 1493. The theme of the paintings may be drawn from the poem, *Punica*, by Silus Italicus, which was well known in antiquity and which humanistic culture restored to fame. In the first panel, Scipione, the sleeping knight, must choose between Venus (pleasure) and Minerva (virtue); in the second, the Graces reward his choice of virtue with the Golden Apples of the Hesperides. The classical origin of this theme brings us back without doubt to the Florentine environment. The composition, which is dominated by a sense of great harmony, is a figurative consequence of the literary theme.

These panels, which were originally attributed to the first period of Raphael's activity, are now thought to have been painted around 1504-1505. By comparing them to one another, we can begin to identify Florentine influences. An analytical rendering of detail distinguishes the first panel, while an abstract quality characterizes the second. The landscape background is deep and spatious and is reduced to broad fields of color. The figures of the three Graces which dominate the foreground are solidly constructed, but they are also modelled by a delicate chiaroscuro.

The *Madonna del Granduca* (1504) in the Palatine Gallery in Florence shows the pre-eminent influence of Leonardo. Its simple composition is a prototype of the

Perugino, The Giving of the Keys.
Rome (Vatican), Sistine Chapel.
This fresco, executed in 1482, is part of the mural decoration of the Sistine Chapel. It is considered one of Perugino's masterpieces. Critics claim that its composition may have been a precedent for that of Raphael's Marriage of the Virgin.

Opposite page: Marriage of the Virgin.
Milan, Brera Museum.
This panel, signed and dated 1504, was executed for the church of San Francesco in Città di Castello. Although the painter's style echoes that of Perugino, the perfection of the composition is wholly his own.

11

future Madonnas of Raphael's last Florentine period. The two figures of the Virgin and Child emerge from a dark background (an element evidently derived from Leonardo), bound together by a sweet sentiment which derives largely from the gesture of the Child who, while looking toward the spectator, presses against his Mother. The painting belonged to the XVII century Florentine painter, Carlo Dolci, and then to Grand Duke Ferdinando III of Lorena, from whom its name derives.

The *Small Cowper Madonna*, today in the National Gallery in Washington, is a more analytical variant of the homogeneous and resolute group of the *Madonna del Granduca*. Here the painter expresses the influence of Leonardo in a broad, soft landscape. This landscape contains a small church with a cylindrical dome, which may be an allusion to Bramante's architecture. According to Venturi, it recalls the church of San Bernardino in Urbino. The painting is generally dated 1503-1505.

The *St. Michael* and *St. George and the Dragon* in the Louvre, and the *St. George* of the National Gallery in Washington are bound together both by their subject —an armed youth fighting a dragon—and by stylistic elements. All three are assigned to the Florentine period and echo those stimuli which Raphael received from the great masters who worked in Florence or whose paintings were visible there. The influence of Leonardo—whose fighting warriors from the *Battle of Anghiari* (1505) in the Palazzo della Signoria provided an extraordinary example of martial art (the painting deteriorated very rapidly because of shortcomings in Leonardo's experimental technique and so is no longer visible)—predominates in these works. But references to Flemish painting—particularly that of Hyeronimus Bosch (the glaring light and humanoid monsters which populate the *St. Michael* are characteristic of Bosch)—suggest the environment of Urbino, where Northern influences were still quite alive. Raphael's imagination, which is particularly developed in the details of the *St. Michael*, is more balanced in the figure of the Archangel, the focus of the entire composition. This sense of balance and composure is developed further in the other two panels, where the landscape, still of Umbrian derivation, accentuates the serenity of the figures notwithstanding the dramatic character of the subject. Certain luministic elements, like the reflections of light on the armor in the Washington *St. George*, foreshadow the compositions of the Vatican "Stanze" (compare the *Liberation of St. Peter*). These small panels are indicative of a moment in which the painter gathers the stylistic fruits of what he has assimilated so far and, at the same time, poses pictorial problems which will be developed in the future.

The *Portrait of a Young Man with an Apple* (1505) in the Uffizi has been associated with these paintings. It is difficult to perceive the hand of the artist in the face which, although beautifully drawn, lacks the physiognomic characteristics which typify Raphael's subjects. But the overall attention to the analytical effects of Flemish art can lead us to attribute the work to Raphael, since his attention is turned to the production of this school precisely in these years. Furthermore, the compositional harmony which is a principal element of Raphael's art is visible throughout the compact forms of the solidly conceived portrait. The subject has been associated with Francesco Maria Della Rovere, and possibly correctly: the portrait reached Florence with the

Della Rovere patrimony in 1631 with the marriage of Vittoria Della Rovere to the future Grand Duke Ferdinando II.

Another important aspect of Raphael's Florentine stay is the compositional evolution which his painting underwent. Perugino's compositions—like those of all Quattrocento masters—were based on linear rhythms. In Florence Raphael transformed his compositional type in a constructive-monumental sense. This transformation is recognizable mainly in the human figures, who are still harmonically enclosed in geometric schemes and accompanied by a clear daylight in the background.

An example of his ability to resolve natural elements in a synthetic vision which transcends particular situations is the female portrait called *La Donna Gravida* in the Pitti Gallery, Florence. The subject is a pregnant woman, conscious of her motherhood, who looks intensely toward the spectator, with her hand on her abdomen. The portrait is finely balanced. Solid forms are reduced to pure spherical volumes, overlaid with carefully chosen colors. The sense of color which this painting shows will be used again by Raphael in his portrait of Cardinal Fedra Inghirami.

The same conceptual content underlies the *Woman with a Unicorn* in the Borghese Gallery, Rome. This painting, which shows a young woman holding a small unicorn, was discovered during a restoration in 1930. Until then it had been covered by the image of a female saint with the iconographic attributes of St. Catherine of Alexandria. Present day critics attribute the work to Raphael, referring it to 1505 and to the Florentine environment. It can, in fact, be inserted among the portraits of that period, for it represents an apex in the artist's stylistic development. The fullness of the well constructed figure is set well apart from a vast landscape background, inspired by Leonardo but executed with the clarity typical of Raphael.

Leonardo's influence is particularly strong in *the Blessing Christ* in the Tosio-Martinengo Museum in Brescia. Here Christ is shown emerging from the tomb. He is no longer an object of compassion, as in 14th and 15th century panels. Rather, he is depicted as the Resurrected Christ; he still bears the symbols of the Passion, the crown of thorns and the marks of the nails which bound his hands and feet to the Cross. Every element of the artist's experience with Perugino has by now been abandoned. The figure displays a smoothness of surface and a soft chairoscuro modelling which clearly surpass the abilities of Raphael's Umbrian master.

The controversial *Self Portrait* in the Uffizi is very similar to the *Blessing Christ*, but its poor state of conservation has prevented critics from attributing it objectively and definitively to Raphael. Nevertheless, many art historians consider it a work from the Florentine period. The soft light which pervades the portrait certainly recalls Leonardo, but the restless and problematic elements which Leonardo's complex figurative research present are absent. The intense representation of the youth shows no sign of internal tension. On the contrary, it communicates a serene observation of reality through a pictorial rendering rich in synthetic capacity.

The masterpieces of this period are undoubtedly the *Portraits of Agnolo and Maddalena Doni* in Palazzo Pitti. The merchant, Agnolo Doni, married Maddalena Strozzi in 1503, but Raphael's portraits (which remained in the

Above: Madonna and Child (Connestabile Madonna).
Leningrad, the Hermitage.

Below: The Small Cowper Madonna.
Washington, National Gallery.

Opposite page: The Madonna del Granduca.
Florence, Palazzo Pitti.

family until 1826, when they were acquired by Grand Duke Leopoldo II of Lorene) were probably executed in 1506, the period in which the painter studied the art of Leonardo most closely. The composition of the portraits resembles that of the *Mona Lisa*: the figures are presented in the same way in respect to the picture plane, and their hands, like those of the *Mona Lisa*, are placed on top of one another. But the low horizon of the landscape background, a "distant heir of Piero della Francesca" (Longhi), permits a careful assessment of the human figure by providing a uniform light which defines surfaces and volumes. This relationship between landscape and figure presents a clear contrast to the striking settings of Leonardo, which communicate the impending presence of nature. But the most notable characteristic which distinguishes these portraits from those of Leonardo is the overall sense of serenity which the close attention to the materials of clothes and jewells (which draw one's attention to the couples' wealth) is unable to attenuate. Every element—even those of secondary importance—works together to create a precise balance. These two works, linked not only by the kinship of the subjects, but also by their evident stylistic homogeneity, mark the beginning of Raphael's artistc maturity.

Raphael's stylistic evolution also regards composition, as we have noted. He develops the pyramidal scheme of Leonardo da Vinci and combines it with the monumental compositions of Fra Bartolommeo. His main interest is to maintain formal balance. The controlled use of light is one of the chief tools he uses to achieve this goal. At the same time, he welcomes new tools, among them the figurative motifs of Michelangelo.

Michelangelo's influence on Raphael is evident in the *Madonna of the Meadow*, one of the compositions featuring the Madonna, the infant Christ and young St. John which mark the central point of Raphael's activity in Florence. The pyramidal structure of the figure group again recalls Leonardo (whose cartoon for the *St. Ann* was publicly shown in 1506 in the church of the Santissima Annunziata). But Raphael exerts his own balancing capacity on the Leonardesque volumetric conception, infusing it with the effect of idyllic serenity which characterizes his paintings from this period. The work as a whole is structurally harmonized, from the figure group (dominated by the affectionate figure of the Virgin Mary who supports the Child and glances tenderly at the young St. John) to the vast landscape (made luminous by the mirror-like lake which stretches from one side of the panel to the other). The effects of torsion present in the two children clearly reflect Michelangelo's figurative research. They are also visible in a nearly contemporary panel, called the *La Belle Jardinière*. The *Madonna of the Meadow*, now in the Kunsthistorisches Museum in Vienna, passed from the Taddei family (for whom it was executed) into the Austrian collections in the Settecento. It is signed and dated 1506.

The *Madonna of the Goldfinch*, executed in 1507 for Lorenzo Nasi and now in the Uffizi, is another of Raphael's Florentine panels. It was severely damaged following the partial collapse of the Nasi house in 1547, mentioned by Vasari. It was subsequently restored by Michele di Ridolfo del Ghirlandaio, the son of an artist who was deeply influenced by Raphael. The composition follows that of the *Madonna of the Meadow*, with the essential difference that the children in the *Madonna of*

The Three Graces.
Chantilly, Musée Condè.
The Three Graces probably
formed part of a double panel
whose other component was the
Knight's Dream. The work has
been dated 1504-05. Note the
particularly graceful gesture with
which the three young women
come together to form a harmonic,
but not too tightly closed, group.

the Goldfinch are more firmly united with the central figure of the Virgin. The color is more lively than that of the *Madonna of the Meadow* and foreshadows the coloristic character of Raphael's Roman paintings. The landscape, and particularly the architectural forms it contains, reflects the influence of Flemish art, even though it is still structured in the Umbrian manner. This influence was as alive in Florence as it was in Urbino in the second half of the Quattrocento. It is perhaps most visible in the sloping roofs and tall spires, unusual elements in a Mediterranean landscape. The influence of Michelangelo is again evident in the well structured figure of the infant Christ. It will be even more evident in the works which follow.

The so-called *Belle Jardinière*, now in the Louvre, follows the *Madonna of the Goldfinch* chronologically. Its composition is a mirror image of that of the *Madonna of the Meadow*. The painting was commissioned by Fabrizio Sergardi, a Sienese nobleman, and was left uncompleted by the artist. Nevertheless, it is signed and dated 1507. It was finished by Ridolfo del Ghirlandaio (whose hand is visible mainly in the mantle of the Madonna), and was subsequently acquired by Francis I of France. The painting is known primarily for the harmonic and proportional balancing of the poses of the figures and for the high formal quality which is present in every element, particularly in the face of the Virgin, which served as a model of beauty for generations of artists.

Between Florence and Rome

Among the figurative components which Raphael drew from his Florentine experience (which, as we have seen, was interrupted by frequent trips to Umbria), those which derive from Michelangelo seem most prevalent in his last Florentine works. The work in which Michelangelo's importance to Raphael becomes most evident is the *Entombment*, in the Borghese Gallery in Rome. The panel was painted in 1507 in Perugia for Atalanta Baglioni as a votive offering in memory of her son, Grifonetto, killed in a piazza in Perugia in the course of a family feud. The artist detaches himself both formally and iconographically from traditional representations of the scene. He does not depict the deposition itself, but the carrying of the dead Christ. The protagonists of the scene do not demonstrate their sorrow violently, but are reduced, through the Raphaelesque mode of feeling, to a sort of painful resignation. Critics have pointed out a resemblance between Raphael's *Entombment* and classical bas-reliefs illustrating the carrying of Meleager, a hero of Greek mythology. The vision of space is less geometric than the Florentine vision, and it appears freer and closer to nature. The influence of Michelangelo is strong, however, and can be perceived without doubt in the limp arm of Christ as well as in the female figure at the extreme right. The latter mirrors the figure of the Virgin in the *Doni Tondo*, which Michelangelo had executed between 1504 and 1506. The formal vigor and sense of open space which characterize Michelangelo's painting certainly must have had a profound effect on Raphael.

16

The three compositions of the predella are executed in a delicate monochrome. They represent Faith, Hope and Charity accompanied by small angels who bear objects symbolizing the virtues. The predominance of the human figure is complete in every composition and the sense of harmony is pervasive. Even in the secondary elements of his creations, Raphael does not spare his capacity to use line and pose to create an overall image of complete formal beauty.

Both the main panel and the predella were carried from Perugia to Rome by Pope Paul V and were replaced by a copy executed in 1608. The painting was subsequently included among the works taken by the French troops and was exhibited in Paris in the Napoleonic Museum from 1797 to 1815 when, following the restitutions ordered by the Congress of Vienna, it was returned to Rome.

The *Canigiani Holy Family* in Munich is attributed to the same period as the *Entombment* (1504-1506). The painting's name derives from the Florentine family who owned it before it passed into the Medici collection and then into Germany with the marriage of Anna Maria Lodovica de' Medici to the Palatine Elector. In this work Raphael synthesizes elements drawn from Leonardo and Michelangelo and compounds them with a decisively Northern landscape and delicate coloristic passages dominated by iridescent tones. The pyramid in which the figures are ideally enclosed is still drawn from models provided by Leonardo, but the relationships between the figures, developed through the glances they interchange and through the serene feelings they communicate, carry the composition onto a calmly descriptive plane. The tone of the painting is thus quite different from the tense and restless art of Leonardo. His unsurpassed descriptive capacity permits Raphael to create an image full of human participation and limpid serenity.

The female portrait known as *The Mute Woman* represents a return to the influence of Leonardo. It is the only work of Raphael conserved in his native city. It certainly comes from the Florentine environment, for it was given in trust to the National Gallery of the Marche by the Uffizi, where it had been stored for several hundred years. It was attributed to Raphael only very recently. Leonardo inspires mainly the pose of the figure (whose characteristically crossed hands constitute a very clear reference to the *Mona Lisa*). The neatness of the large areas of color which emerge in lighter tones from the near-black background, and the analytical treatment of the details of the woman's clothing are characteristic of Raphael. The dispersive effect of this attention to detail is fully compensated by the tones of color—used here in a fairly limited range—which unify the composition as a whole.

The stylistic versatility which Raphael demonstrates in contemporary or nearly contemporary works executed for a homogeneous social environment is indicative of his extraordinary technical capacity. This versatility is expressed in a variety of compositional types, which can range from simple forms to more monumental and complex ones; and in conceptual expressions, which are sometimes calm and quiet and sometimes emphatic.

This range of figurative expressions appears in another

Above: St. Michael and the Dragon. Paris, Louvre.

Below: St. George and the Dragon. Paris, Louvre.

*Opposite page: St. George and the Dragon.
Washington, National Gallery.*

work from the Florentine period, the *Madonna del Baldacchino* in Palazzo Pitti. This painting was begun in 1507 for the Dei family and was intended for their chapel in the church of Santo Spirito. The panel's monumental structure derives partially from the Venetian tradition and partially from Fra Bartolommeo. The Venetian influence is visible above all in the setting: the apse of a church which recalls the larger compositions of Giovanni Bellini. The influence of Fra Bartolommeo consists largely in the monumentality and poses of the figures. The semi-circular arrangement of the saints around the Virgin and the unusually excited flying angels who hold open the curtain of the baldachin give the painting a sense of free atmospheric circulation. The figures, all posed differently, prepare a complex of expressions which will find its natural outlet in the large descriptive compositions of the Vatican.

Fra Bartolommeo's influence is particularly clear in the *Large Cowper Madonna* in the National Gallery in Washington. This panel, signed and dated 1508, was executed near the end of Raphael's stay in Florence. The composition is extremely simple and essential; the gesture of the Child, who stretches his hand toward the Virgin while turning his attention toward the spectator, and the gesture with which the Virgin holds the hand to her breast, provide the only signs of life. The sentiment of anxious motherhood which, enriched by greater awareness, will be fully expressed in the *Tempi Madonna* in the Alte Pinakothek of Munich, appears here for the first time. The Virgin, who tenderly presses the Infant to her cheek, is the subject of the painting. But the two figures are conceived as a single group, and this fact dominates the scene's visual impact. The only natural elements are a small strip of landscape and the light blue sky in the background. The Madonna's swollen mantle is meant to indicate movement. The extreme synthesis of the color fields indicates Raphael's idealization of the subject. But the painter's need for formal beauty and the emotional reality of the subject matter are reconciled above all through the affective relationship between Mother and Child. This panel, which critics place in the year 1508, is included among the works executed after Raphael's contact with Florentine art.

The *St. Catherine of Alexandria* in the National Gallery, London, is also assigned to this period. The martyr is shown almost full figure, turned toward the sky in an act of ecstasy which foreshadows the "*devotional* intonation of the large Roman altarpieces" (De Vecchi). The landscape is painted with particular care. Its light shading indicates a residual influence of Leonardo, although the jagged mountains which often characterize Leonardo's landscapes are absent. The delicate modelling of the saint, the light torsion of the body which leans on the wheel of her martyrdom (whose spikes have been reduced to rounded knobs in order to tone down the element of cruelty) fully express the balanced character of Raphael's art. The panel clearly shows the intense formal research which underlies Raphael's figurative creations. He is always careful not to excite emotions which he considers too intense and to mitigate tones and thematic elements in search of a perfect balance between design, color, pose and expression, and between the figurative and ornamental elements.

After having passed most of 1509 in Florence, Raphael prepared to leave for Rome. That he was present

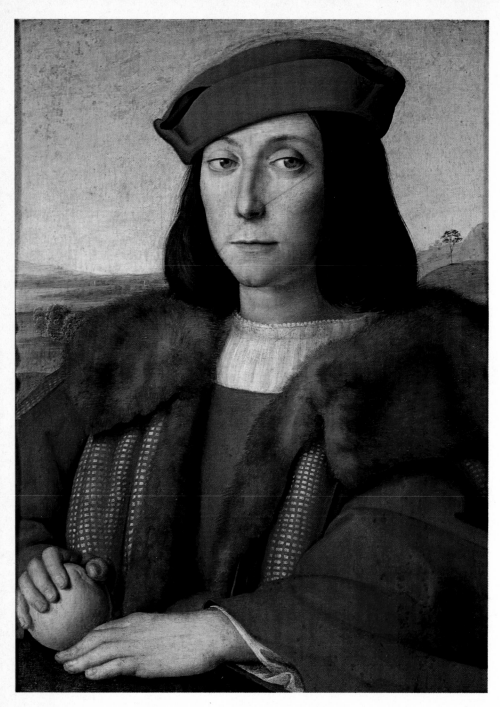

Portrait of a Young Man with
an Apple. Florence, Uffizi.
Formal elements deriving
from Flemish art—for instance,
the careful, analytical
rendering of the subject—have
been found in this intense
portrait. The work may
be dated approximately 1505.

Opposite page: The Woman
with the Unicorn.
Rome, Borghese Gallery.
The addition of details of a
religious-devotional nature
(the palm of martyrdom,
the wheel) changed this profane
portrait into a representation
of St. Catherine of Alexandria.
A careful restoration removed
the additions and brought
back the unicorn,
a symbol of chastity.
The painting is dated 1505-06.

in Perugia for a brief period is certain. There he executed a fresco in the Convent of San Severo which may
be regarded as a prototype of the compositions in the
first frescoes of the Vatican Stanze. The painting, representing the *Holy Trinity and Saints*, consists of two
parts and still shows the influence of Fra Bartolommeo,
although the Umbrian environment causes Raphael to
resume some elements of his experience with Perugino
which had seemed already forgotten.

These works conclude Raphael's Florentine experience.
They clearly demonstrate the stylistic knowledge and
figurative means that he acquired through observing and
frequenting the Tuscan masters.

Julius II Della Rovere was Pope when Raphael arrived
in Rome. The group of humanists, literary figures and
artists which had previously formed at the court of Ur-

bino was reconstructed around his throne. There were
close contacts between the Papal environment and that
of Urbino, for the Della Rovere family dominated both
Urbino and Rome. The Urbinate architect, Donato Bramante (1444-1514), who came to Rome from Lombardy
and whose Tempietto at San Pietro in Montorio was built
along a central plan similar to that which Raphael had
painted in the *Marriage of the Virgin*, was particularly
active. Furthermore, classical antiquity was the object
of new studies and interests during the pontificate of
Julius II. The discovery of the antique sculpture group,
the *Laocoon*, in 1506 was followed by a great deal of
excitement among artists and literary figures. The relo-
cation of this and other statues from the Greek and
Roman periods in the Belvedere Garden in the Vatican
changed the stylistic tendencies of art in Rome. Even

Raphael, who had just arrived in Rome, assimilated certain classical motifs which he believed responsive to his figurative research.

Julius II (Pope from 1503 to 1513) was a complicated and dynamic personality. After having broken up the rival Borgia faction, he headed the so-called Holy League, whose goal was to drive the French out of the territories which bordered on the Papal States. This was accomplished with the aid of several Italian principalities. Julius' military undertakings were associated with an extraordinary wealth of initiatives in the re-organization of the state: he directed the re-ordering of the Papal finances (which Borgia expenditures had reduced to a deplorable state) and restored confidence in the money by minting new silver *giuli* whose nominal and effective values were guaranteed to correspond. Much energy was also dedicated to city planning. New neighborhoods and streets were created (among them, the famous Via Giulia) and an ambitious project for the renewal of St. Peter's was begun. This creative fervor in the artistic field attracted the most famous artists of the time, from Antonio da Sangallo to Jacopo Sansovino, from Bramante to Pintoricchio, from Lotto to Michelangelo and from Si-

gnorelli to Raphael himself. Their presence contributed to the remaking of Rome. The political, social and demographic decadence which had afflicted the city in the Middle Ages were gradually and laboriously eliminated, and Rome became the most important cultural center in Italy.

Raphael in Rome. The Early Years

Raphael's first major enterprise in Rome was the decoration of the Stanza della Segnatura. He started work in June 1509, one year after Michelangelo had begun the vaults of the Sistine Chapel, another great pictorial cycle commissioned by Pope Julius. Both these works have a clear religious content, but their aims are different. The Sistine Chapel was intended for liturgical celebrations. Its ceiling is populated by figures who are independent of the environment and of nature and who are capable of recreating the complex and tormented expression of man's most deeply felt faith. The Stanza della Segnatura was a courtroom: its purpose was the

Above, left: Portrait of Agnolo Doni. Florence, Uffizi.
Raphael's ability as a portrait painter is clearly
expressed in the solid, coherent forms
of this panel, dated 1506.

Above, right: Portrait of Maddalena Strozzi Doni.
Florence, Uffizi.
The same formal elements which characterize
the portrait of Angelo Doni are also present
in that of his wife, Maddalena Strozzi. Critics believe
the Portrait of Maddalena Strozzi Doni to have been
executed slightly later than that of Agnolo Doni.

Below: Self-portrait. Florence, Uffizi.
Tradition attributes this painting to Raphael.
Although Raphael is undoubtedly the subject,
modern critics are uncertain as to whether
or not it is a self-portrait.

Opposite page: La Donna Gravida. Florence, Uffizi.
The unusual subject matter does not interfere
with Raphael's ability to create a harmonious
composition. Note, for instance, the masterful
correspondence of volumetric forms. The panel
is dated 1505-1506.

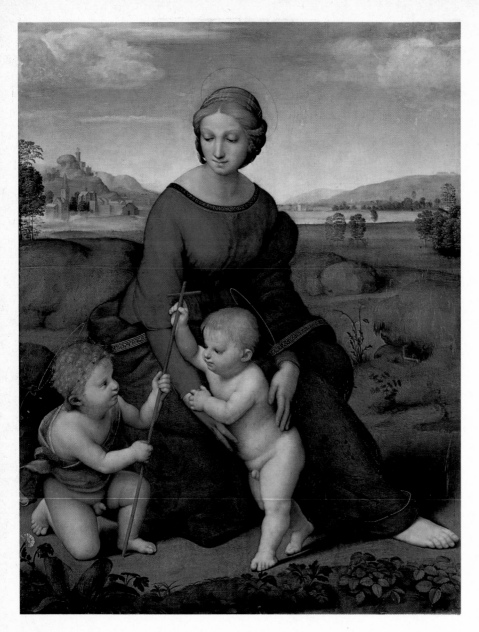

administration of temporal power. Its decoration—harmonious settings populated by sacred and profane characters—reflected a Church by this time invested with worldly powers and occupied with their administration.

Julius II had commissioned the decoration of this room to the most well known painters active in Rome: the Sienese, Baldassare Peruzzi; the Vercellese, (but naturalized Sienese) Antonio Bazzi, called "il Sodoma"; the Lombard, Bramantino; and the Venetian, Lorenzo Lotto. But Raphael's program excited the Pope so much that —according to Vasari—the works already begun by the other artists were demolished and the entire cycle was placed in Raphael's hands.

The illustrative program of the paintings of the Stanza della Segnatura, which combined antique thought with Christian humanistic re-interpretations, was certainly not conceived by Raphael. It is certain, however, that his abilities as an illustrator immediately allowed him to give visual form to the complex doctrine which the subject matter implied. The accompanying diagram explains the content of the cycle:

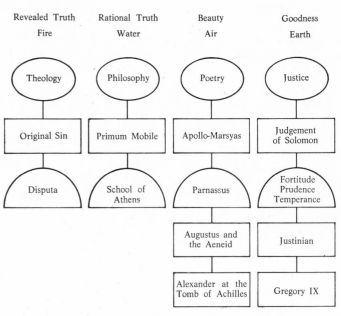

Revealed Truth Fire	Rational Truth Water	Beauty Air	Goodness Earth
Theology	Philosophy	Poetry	Justice
Original Sin	Primum Mobile	Apollo-Marsyas	Judgement of Solomon
Disputa	School of Athens	Parnassus	Fortitude Prudence Temperance
		Augustus and the Aeneid	Justinian
		Alexander at the Tomb of Achilles	Gregory IX

Seen together, the paintings can be considered a synthesis of motifs which illustrate "the agreement between ancient world and Christian spirituality" (Chastel), since it places the virtue of the religious tradition and the spiritual activities of man side by side in a cosmological environment (that is, an environment that refers to the elements which constitute the universe). To achieve this synthesis, Raphael chooses exemplary episodes from the Bible (the Original Sin and the Judgement of Solomon), from classical mythology (Apollo and Marsyas) and from the Aristotelian philosophical conception reconsidered in the light of humanistic Platonism (the Primum Mobile, the highest of heavens, set in motion directly by God).

Humanistic-Platonic philosophy, which is basically the the thought of Plato adapted to the Christian tradition by the philosophers of the early Renaissance, inspires the entire cycle. According to the most recent studies, the cycle represents the ideas of *truth* (both the truth revealed by the Christian religion and the rational truth of classical philosophical speculation), *virtue* (personified by ecclesiastic and civil law and symbolized by the Virtues) and *beauty* (as it is expressed in Poetry).

The realization of the frescoes for the Stanza della Segnatura involved numerous preparatory drawings. These drawings indicate the immense amount of creative energy which underlie the compositions. In fact, Raphael was immediately recognized by the literary figures, thinkers and artists who populated Rome as a personality capable of interpreting the ideas of the intellectual speculation of his time in extraordinarily balanced figurative forms. In the vaults and wall panels, he adapts himself to the work already begun by others. His most original creations are in the large lunettes, where he fully integrates the suggested theme and its formal realization.

The first composition Raphael executed is the so-called *Disputa* or *Disputation of the Holy Sacrament*, the traditional name for what is really an *Adoration of the Sacrament*. The painting is built around the monstrance containing the consacrated Host, located on the altar. Figures representing the Triumphant Church and the Militant Church are arranged in two semicircles, one above the other, and venerate the Host. God the Father, bathed in celestial glory, blesses the crowd of Biblical and ecclesiastical figures from the top of the composition. Immediately below, the resurrected Christ sits on a throne of clouds between the Virgin (bowed in adoration) and St. John the Baptist (who, according to iconographic tradition, points to Christ). Prophets and saints of the Old and New Testament are seated around this central group on a semicircular bank of clouds similar to that which constitutes the throne of Christ. They form a composed and silent crowd and, although they are painted with large fields of color, the figures are highly individuated. At the bottom of the picture space, inserted in a vast landscape dominated by the altar and the eucharistic sacrifice, are saints, popes, bishops, priests and the mass of the faithful. They represent the Church which has acted, and which continues to act, in the world, and which contemplates the glory of the Trinity with the eyes of the mind. Following a fifteenth century tradition, Raphael has placed portraits of famous personalities, both living and dead, among the figures of this crowd. Bramante leans on the ballustrade at left; the young man standing near him has been identified as Francesco Della Rovere; Pope Julius II, who per-

sonifies Gregory the Great, is seated near the altar. Dante is visible on the right, distinguished by a crown of laurel. The presence of Savonarola seems strange, but may be explained by the fact that Julius II revoked Pope Alexander VI's condemnation of Savonarola (Julius was an adversary of Alexander, who was a Borgia). The structure of the composition is characterized by extreme clarity and simplicity, which Raphael achieved through sketches, studies and drawings containing notable differences in pose. References to other artists are visible throughout the composition (the young Francesco Maria Della Rovere, for example, possesses a Leonardo-like physiognomy). But the layout, the gestures and the poses are original products of Raphael's research, which here reaches a degree of admirable balance and high expressive dignity.

Toward the end of 1509, Raphael began work on the wall opposite the *Disputa*. This second fresco, entitled the *School of Athens*, represents the truth acquired through reason. Raphael does not entrust his illustration to allegorical figures, as was customary in the 14th and 15th centuries. Rather, he groups the solemn figures of thinkers and philosophers together in a large, grandiose architectural framework. This framework is characterized by a high dome, a vault with lacunar ceiling and pilasters. It is probably inspired by late Roman architecture or—as most critics believe—by Bramante's project for the new St. Peter's, which is itself a symbol of the synthesis of pagan and Christian philosophies. According to Chastel, it is thus "the only symbol capable of representing the work of the intelligence."

The figures who dominate the composition do not crowd the environment, nor are they suffocated by it. Rather, they underline the breadth and depth of the architectural structures. The protagonists—Plato, represented with a white beard (some people identify this solemn old man with Leonardo) and Aristotle—are both characterized by a precise and meaningful pose. "The horizontal gesture of Aristotle symbolizes the organization of the world through Ethics and the vertical gesture of Plato represents the movement of cosmological thought which rises from the sensible world to its ideal principle" (Chastel). Raphael's descriptive capacity, in contrast to that visible in the allegories of preceding painters, is such that "the figures do not pay homage to or group around the symbols of knowledge; they do not form a parade. They move, act, teach, discuss and become excited" (Venturi).

The painting celebrates classical thought, but it is also dedicated to the liberal arts, symbolized by the statues of Apollo and Minerva. Grammar, Arithmetic and Music are personified by figures located in the foreground, at the left. Geometry and Astronomy are personified by the figures in the foreground, at the right. Behind them stand characters representing Rhetoric and Dialectic. Some of the ancient philosophers bear the features of Raphael's contemporaries. Bramante is shown as Euclid (in the foreground, at the right, leaning over a tablet and holding a compass). Leonardo is, as we said, probably shown as Plato. Francesco Maria Della Rovere appears once again near Bramante, dressed in white. Michelangelo, sitting on the stairs and leaning on a block of marble, is represented as Heraclitus. A close examination of the intonaco shows that Heraclitus was the last figure painted when the fresco was com-

pleted, in 1511. The allusion to Michelangelo is probably a gesture of homage to the artist, who had recently
unveiled the frescoed ceiling of the Sistine Chapel. Raphael—at the extreme right, with a dark hat—and
his friend, Sodoma, are also present (they exemplify
the glorification of the fine arts and they are posed on
the same level as the liberal arts). The fresco achieved
immediate success. Its beauty and its thematic unity
were universally accepted. The enthusiasm with which
it was received was not marred by reservations, as was
the public reaction to the Sistine Ceiling.

Raphael began the third composition for the Stanza

della Segnatura at the end of 1509 or the beginning
of 1510. It represents *Parnassus*, the dwelling place
of Apollo and the Muses and the home of poetry, according to classical myth. Apollo plays a lyre (an anachro-
nism which, according to some, was invented to symbolize the perpetual value of the poetic message). He
sits under a laurel grove with the nine Muses (who per-
sonify the nine types of art). Classical poets are represented in a harmonic ascending and descending movement from left to right. Some of them are portraits of
contemporary or historical figures: Petrarch is recognizable in the group in the left foreground; so is Sappho,

The Entombment. Rome, Borghese Gallery.
The panel is signed and dated 1507. Conceived as
a votive image, it was commissioned by Atalanta Baglioni
for the church of San Francesco al Prato in Perugia,
in memory of her son, Grifonetto. The painting
contains numerous motifs drawn from Michelangelo.
It is the last major work executed
by Raphael before leaving Florence for Rome.

Opposite page: The Pious Women
(detail of the Entombment).
Raphael always limits the expression of pain to
'medium' tones consistent with the emotional balance
which he strives to maintain in his paintings.

32

who holds a scroll bearing her name; Ennius is seated above them, listening to the song of the blind Homer (who appears as a protagonist, like Apollo); behind him stands Dante, who had also appeared in the *Disputa* as a theologist, evidently because of the doctrinal content of the *Divine Comedy*. Some see the portrait of Michelangelo in the bearded figure immediately to the right of the central group, but the figure is more readily identified with Tebaldeo or Castiglione, for the scene is, after all, a celebration of poetry. Compositional harmony and visual counterpoint characterize the fresco: the groups of figures are bound together by continuous lines and the single characters are represented in opposed but corresponding poses. Although the *Parnassus* lacks the high originality of the *School of Athens*, it demonstrates Raphael's illustrative ability. It is enriched by classical elements which must have held great appeal for a cultural class excited by the recent archaeological discoveries. Thus we must add Raphael's capacity to interpret contemporary taste to his genuine artistic skills.

The lunette containing the *Cardinal Virtues* (which represent "Good") is built around an allegorical theme. The volumetric modelling of the figures suggests the influence of Michelangelo. The relationship that binds the three figures together is clear and harmonic. Fortitude, dressed in armor, sits in the shade of an oak tree. Prudence is placed on the highest step of the base. She has two faces: one of a young woman who looks at her reflection in a mirror handed to her by a winged putto; the other, of an old man, the symbol of old age, of which prudence is the chief quality. Finally, Temperance is represented holding a pair of reins. The allegory was intended to include the figure of Justice as well. But Justice, being considered superior to the other virtues from a hierarchical point of view, is represented separately in one of the medallions of the vault. Three winged genii symbolize the theological virtues (Charity, gathering the fruits of the oak; Hope, in the center with a flaming torch; and Faith, at the extreme right, pointing toward the sky). Two additional putti complete the composition, "giving the whole scene a free and graceful movement" (De Vecchi).

After the completion of the Stanza della Segnatura, Raphael began the decoration of the adjacent room, afterwards called the Stanza di Eliodoro, after the subject of one of the works painted there. The cycle was painted between September 1511 and June 1514. Julius II died during this period and his successor, Leo X (Giovanni de' Medici, son of Lorenzo the Magnificent) influenced the last scenes to be completed.

In the meanwhile, Raphael had had contact with the art of Sebastiano del Piombo. Sebastiano had come to Rome in 1511 and had worked with Raphael in the villa of the wealthy Sienese banker, Agostino Chigi (the villa was later called La Farnesina). The intense colors of the Venetian artist's paintings had attracted Raphael. The result of this contact can be seen in the richer range of color which Raphael used in these scenes.

The vaults of the ceiling represent episodes of divine intervention in the history of Israel (the Burning Bush, the Announcement of the Flood to Noah, Jacob's Dream, the Sacrifice of Isaac). The theme of the room is the presence of God in the history of the Church (including *Heliodorus' Expulsion from the Temple* [Maccabees, 3:24-27] and other episodes.) It commemorates the conquest of

Opposite page: The Theological Virtues. Rome, Vatican Museum.

Above: The Canigiani Holy Family and a detail of the landscape. Munich, Alte Pinakothek.

*Above: Madonna del Baldacchino and detail
of an angel. Florence, Palazzo Pitti.*

*Opposite page: The Mute Woman.
Urbino, Galleria Nazionale delle Marche.*

Palestine by the Hellenistic kingdom of the Syrian Seleucides. The other episodes refer to the Middle Ages (for example, the *Mass at Bolsena* and *Attila's meeting with Leo the Great*) or to the early years of the Christian Church (e.g., the *Liberation of St. Peter*). Therefore the cycle is mainly descriptive. Raphael develops it with those characteristics of dignity and grandiosity which by now are his trademarks. He enhances his compositions by breaking up the symmetry and the enclosed rhythm of the Stanza della Segnatura with more lively and colorful effects.

These trends appear first in the *Expulsion of Heliodorus*. The focus of the scene is no longer at the center. Rather, it is shifted to the right. Here Heliodorus and his followers, profaning the Temple of Jerusalem, are driven out by an armed rider and by two running figures. In the center, the expanse of the wide nave, illuminated by the reflections of light in the vault, is a more effective space-determining motif than the large patches of blue sky which appeared through the coffered ceiling of the *School of Athens*. At the extreme left, Pope Julius II dominates the bystanders, and he reappears in subsequent scenes as well. Raphael's new compositional formula, so unexpected after the extremely controlled compositions of the Stanza della Segnatura, is visible in all its dynamic evidence from this fresco onward.

Another exceptional event is represented after the *Expulsion of Heliodorus*. It is the basis of the Catholic ceremony of the *Corpus Domini*.

In 1263 a priest from Bohemia, during a pilgrimage to Rome, saw blood dripping from the Chalice onto the Corporal cloth while celebrating Mass in Bolsena. This was interpreted as a supernatural answer to the priest's skepticism regarding the transubstantiation. The cloth, as proof of the miracle, was transferred to the neighboring city of Orvieto to be preserved in the Cathedral. The church was rebuilt (in its present form) to honor the occasion. Raphael represents the priest, the protagonist of the event, close to the center of the composition. As he raises the Host, two devotees lean over the semicircular screen which forms the background of the scene. This is a further attempt by Raphael to represent figures in a more dynamic way. Some critics believe he was inspired by Lorenzo Lotto, who was among the artists who had begun to paint the Stanza della Segnatura before his intervention. Pope Julius appears at the right of the scene, a symbol of the ecclesiastical authority's presence during, and approval of, the miracle. The Pope's attendants stand one step below and behind him. The asymmetry of the composition regards time as well as space: the excitement of the figures at the left represents a reaction to the supernatural event, which they witness; the stillness of the Pope and his attendants indicates their *spiritual* presence, achieved through a meditative evocation of the event.

Raphael's assistants played a greater role in painting the Heliodorus cycle than in the Stanza della Segnatura. This is clearly a consequence of the growing number of commissions which the Romans granted to Raphael. The hand of Giulio Romano, one of his most faithful pupils, is visible in the episode showing the *Liberation of St. Peter*. The composition of this fresco clearly reflects the order and unity of the *Mass of Bolsena*. But the story is broken down into three distinct episodes, taken from the *Acts of the Apostles*. The first shows the Dismay

of the Guards; the second shows the appearance of the Angel of Freedom in the saint's cell; the third, the bewildered Peter led by the hand by the divine messenger. The barred cell is on an upper level (like the altar in the *Mass*) and is reached by steps to the left and right. A group of agitated figures occupies the stairway at the left. Here, a soldier—whose armor reflects the light of the moon—asks his sleepy and bewildered comrades what is going on. At the right, the angel leads the stunned and still-sleepy St. Peter past another sleeping guard. Here, for the first time, Raphael attempts a "night effect," using both the natural light of the moon and the autonomous light of the angel. This painting is the last fresco that can be attributed to Raphael with certainty. The large cycles which follow (except for the *Sibyls* of Santa Maria della Pace) are entrusted mainly to assistants.

In the last episode of the Stanza di Eliodoro, Raphael returns to the symmetrical compositional type of the Stanza della Segnatura. The painting represents Pope Leo the Great who, with the assistance of God, prevented the Huns from attacking Rome. The figure of the Pope on horseback is a portrait of Leo X. It was originally intended to represent Julius II, but the Della Rovere Pope died before the completion of the cycle, and his portrait was substituted by that of his successor. The scene is divided into two parts: at the left the Pope and his attendants, poised and solemn, offer a gesture of peace to the Huns. Below them, on foot, Saints Peter and Paul brandish a sword. At the right Attila and his

Left: The Large Cowper Madonna. Washington, National Gallery. The panel, signed and dated 1508, belonged to the Niccolini family of Florence. Its simple composition became a model for early 16th century Florentine painters.

Right: The Tempi Madonna. Munich, Alte Pinakothek. This panel, generally dated to 1508, is one of Raphael's most successful efforts to combine human sentiment and idealized form.

Opposite page: St. Catherine of Alexandria. London, National Gallery. The torsion of the martyr-saint's body is a clear reference to the art of Michelangelo. The figure evokes an intense religious feeling, even though it is painted with typical Raphaelesque restraint.

Opposite page: Stanza della Segnatura. Rome, Vatican.
Raphael's first commission in Rome was the fresco
decoration of the rooms of Pope Julius II's
Vatican apartments. Sources and documents state
that the Stanza della Segnatura, or high Papal court,
was painted between 1508 and 1511. The cycle
follows a precise iconographic program.
It combines motifs drawn from the Christian
tradition and from classical antiquity.

The Disputa (Stanza della Segnatura).
The composition (which actually represents the Adoration
of the Sacrament) is a grandiose transposition
of Catholic doctrine, based on the representation
of Christ, the Eucharest, and the militant
and triumphant Church.

Following pages: The School of Athens
(Stanza della Segnatura).
In a grandiose architectural setting (which reflects
Bramante's project for St. Peter's) the great figures
of classical philosophy (who symbolize human reason's
search for Truth) think, write, and talk among themselves.

attendants, also on horseback, listen with dignity. Below
them, an armed foot soldier counterbalances the figures
of the two Saints. In the background are Rome and
Mount Mario, on which a fire is blazing.

This episode is clearly more fragmentary and dispersive
than the other frescoes of the cycle. Many critics attribute this weakness to the extensive participation of Raphael's pupils, led by Giulio Romano.

The room of the *Fire in the Borgo* where, from 1514
to 1517, Raphael's workshop illustrated historical episodes in which the protagonists are the Popes named Leo,
completes our examination of the Vatican cycles. This
room contains episodes like the *Fire in the Borgo*, in
which a miracle performed by Pope Leo IV caused a
fire raging in Rome to be extinguished; the *Battle of
Ostia*, in which the Saracens were lost in a storm at
sea, presumably because of the presence of Leo IV; and
the *Coronation of Charlemagne* by Pope Leo III on
Christmas Day, 799. Here the illustration of themes
drawn from the past mixes with the celebration of the
political projects of the present Pope, in this case Leo
X's reconciliation with France. The fourth subject, the
Oath of Leo III, anticipates the numerous representations
of Popes and bishops in assizes which became common
during the Counter Reformation in the late 16th century.

The *Fire in the Borgo* is the most complex of the
four episodes. It is full of citations of classical antiquity,

Above, left: Heraclitus
(detail of the School of Athens).
The thoughtful figure of Heraclitus, painted in 1511,
was the last figure to be added to the composition.
Many critics believe it to be a portrait of Michelangelo,
who completed the Sistine ceiling in the same year.

Right: Euclid
(detail of the School of Athens).
The Greek thinker, who stands over a tablet
containing a geometric drawing,
bears the features of Bramante.

Below: Pythagoras
(detail of the School of Athens).
The Greek philosopher and mathematician is shown
in the act of writing in a large book while an assistant
hands him a drawing symbolizing his research.

Mt. Parnassus (Stanza della Segnatura).
The composition represents the mythical home of Apollo
and the Muses, inhabited by famous poets from classical
antiquity, the Middle Ages and the Renaissance.
The theme of the fresco is 'Beauty', as expressed
by poetry. The fresco was painted in 1510-11.

of medieval architecture of the time of the affirmation of the Church, and of themes used by contemporary artists. It celebrates the intercession of Leo IV, by whose grace a fire which spread through the Borgo, a popular section of Rome near the Basilica of St. Peter, was extinguished. The structure of the composition is complex: two colonnades of clear classical derivation define a square. The Pope, who again bears the features of Leo X, blesses the frightened crowd from a gallery located beyond the colonnades. The façade of Old Saint Peter's appears behind him, in the extreme background. The term 'scenography' can appropriately be applied to this painting. Clearly, Raphael was concentrating on richer, more varied, but less harmonious compositional solutions than those of his previous paintings. The figure groups express great formal beauty, but they lack harmonious relationships and remain pure examples of episodical representation. The group in the left foreground, for example (made up of an old man on the shoulders of a young man, and a child) may be drawn from the episode of the *Aeneid* in which Aeneas escapes with his father, Anchises and his son, Ascanius. The woman with children in the center of the fresco and the water carrier at the right, whose clothes blow in the wind, represent similar stereotypes. The nude descending from the wall at left recalls the heroic figures of Michelangelo. Notwithstanding these limitations, the scene is highly effective and demonstrates Raphael's skill as an illustrator, although, as the critics maintain, it was executed largely by his pupils.

Opposite page; above, left:Dante Alighieri
(detail of Mt. Parnassus).

Opposite page; above, right: The Muses
(detail of Mt. Parnassus).

Opposite page, below: The Cardinal Virtues
(Stanza della Segnatura).
Fortitude, Prudence and Temperance, the cardinal virtues,
appear here accompanied by winged genii which
allude to Hope, Charity and Faith.

Above: The Expulsion of Heliodorus.
Rome, Vatican, Stanza di Eliodoro.
The second room, frescoed between 1511 and 1514,
illustrates divine interventions in the history
of the Jews and of the Church. Its name derives
from the Biblical episode of Heliodorus, who was
expelled from the Temple of Jerusalem
(during the Syrian domination of Palestine)
by three young men who appeared miraculously.

Below: The Priest, Anias, in prayer
(detail of the Expulsion of Heliodorus).
The high priest, in the shadows of the temple,
invokes divine aid against the intruders. The detail
exemplifies the luministic effects which Raphael
uses to heighten the dramatic effect of action
in the Stanza di Eliodoro.

Raphael After the Vatican Stanze. The Last Years

The fame of his fresco cycles brought Raphael numerous other commissions in Rome. Some of these were executed at the same time as the monumental cycles of the Vatican Stanze.

One of the masterpieces of this period is the *Portrait of a Cardinal* today in the Prado in Madrid. This painting was once considered a work of the mature painter. But it has recently been dated 1510-1511 on the basis of the composition, which resembles those of the *Portraits of Agnolo and Maddalena Doni* and the *Mute Woman*. The pose is identical: the figure is turned three-quarters out and the arm nearest the viewer defines the lower limit of the picture space.

Raphael returns to the representation of the Virgin and Child with St. John in the *Madonna del Duca D'Alba*. The composition of this tondo is extremely simple. The pyramidal scheme is expanded in width. The cold and resonant colors contrast with the delicate greens and light blues of the broad landscape background. Small, symmetrically arranged flowers provide centers of color against the ochre tones of the ground. The Virgin's eyes are symbolically fixed on the cross made of sticks which St. John (who is the Precursor of Christ) and the infant Christ both hold. The vigorous modelling

The Mass of Bolsena (Stanza di Eliodoro).
The episode represents the miracle which caused blood to drip from the Chalice onto the Corporal cloth during a mass celebrated by a Bohemian priest who doubted the doctrine of transubstantiation.
Pope Julius II and his throne-bearers are present at the extreme right of the painting.

Opposite page: The Throne-bearers (detail of the Mass of Bolsena).
The controlled realism evident in the portrait-like faces and detailed costumes of the Pope's throne-bearers (who kneel behind the Pope, at right) exemplifies Raphael's extraordinary attention to detail.

of her drapery may be inspired by Michelangelo. But, as Venturi notes, "the pure features, the radiant open eyes, translate the solemn...language of Michelangelo into the melodic language of Raphael." The work is roughly dated 1511.

The Sienese Banker, Agostini Chigi, played a very important role in the cultural and artistic activities which flourished around Julius II, as we have already pointed out. His house was built on the periphery of Rome in 1509-1510, and was designed as a model of luxury and elegance. He commissioned the most famous artists of the time, Baldassarre Peruzzi, Sebastiano Luciani (later called Sebastiano del Piombo) and Raphael himself to decorate it. All three painted frescoes based on classical mythology in Chigi's house (which was later acquired by the Farnese family and was called "the Farnesina"). Raphael illustrated a theme from the Greek poet, Theocrates, on the walls of the loggia (or porch), in a painting which combines the vitality of pagan narrative with his unusual compositional harmony. Galatea, the sea-nymph, rushes forward on a dolphin-drawn chariot. Her head is turned to one side and her glance is directed over her shoulder toward the *amorini* or cupids who fly above her, bows drawn. A crowd of sea-nymphs and Tritons —fantastic creatures, half man and half fish—surround her. The powerful nudes possess the energy of Michelangelo, but the soft modelling of the winged cupids is peculiar to Raphael.

The Liberation of St. Peter
(Stanza di Eliodoro).
This episode, drawn from the Acts of the Apostles, takes place at night. The light of the moon and the aura of the angel who miraculously leads the Apostle from his prison cell illuminate the scene.

Left: Angel
(detail of the Liberation of St. Peter).
The divine messenger, shown in full light in the deep
shadow of the prison, bends over the sleeping Apostle
and illuminates the armed figure of the guard at right.

Right: Guards
(detail of the Liberation of St. Peter).
Flashes of light on the guard's armor heightens
the dramatic effect of this scene, which shows
the surprise and bewilderment caused
by the unexpected freeing of the Apostle.

Agostino Chigi later commissioned other works to Raphael: the *Psyche*, also in the Farnesina; the *Sibyls* in the church of Santa Maria della Pace; and the tondo in the church of Santa Maria del Popolo.

A new fresco occupied Raphael during the period 1511-1512: the *Prophet Isaiah* painted for Giovanni Goritz of Luxemberg, Head Chancellor of the Papal Court. That the work was commissioned by a foreigner is indicative of the extraordinary fame that Raphael had acquired. This powerful but composed prophet and the putti who surround him echo Michelangelo's figures in the *Sistine Ceiling*. Nonetheless, the putti, whose glances and poses are enlivened by a strong spiritual tension, are transformed by Raphael into tender and formally controlled children. Even the action of the wind that blows Isaiah's mantle is a life-giving device rather than an expression of dramatic feeling. The dedicatory inscription in Greek (which alludes to Saint Ann, patron of Goritz) and the Hebrew scroll which the Prophet holds, reflect the learned environment in which the work was conceived.

The solemn forms of the Vatican Stanze, the Farnesina frescoes and the *Isaiah* appear again in two large panels representing the *Madonna in Glory*. The first was executed for Sigismondo de' Conti in 1511-1512 and is usually called the *Madonna of Foligno*. The second, dated 1513-1514, is called the *Sistine Madonna*.

Raphael's pictorial research had been enriched by the

luministic solutions of the *Expulsion of Heliodorus* and the *Liberation of St. Peter*. These pictorial devices reappear in the *Madonna of Foligno*, presently located in the Vatican Museum. The Madonna and Child, borne by a cloud of angels and framed by an orange disk, dominate the group of saints below them, which also contains the donor. This group includes—from left to right—St. John the Baptist, St. Francis, Sigismondo de' Conti and St. Jerome. A small angel at the center of the composition holds a small plaque which was originally intended to carry the dedicatory inscription. The painting was commissioned to commemorate a miracle in which the donor's house in Foligno was struck by lightning but was not damaged or—according to another version—was struck by a projectile which fell during the seige of Foligno. The stormy atmosphere of the landscape background and the flash of lightning (or explosion) which strikes the Chigi palace (visible at the left) illustrate the legend. The strong characterization of the figures, the volumetric fullness of the putti and the refined chairoscuro distinguish the panel (which was taken as loot by Napoleon's army in 1799 and returned in 1815) as a work of the mature artist.

The canvas with the Virgin, Child and Saints Sixtus and Barbara, usually called the *Sistine Madonna* (now in the Dresden Museum), is characterized by an imaginary space created by the figures themselves. The figures stand on a bed of clouds, framed by heavy curtains which open to either side. The painting was probably intended to decorate the tomb of Pope Julius II, for Pope Sixtus was the patron saint of the Della Rovere family and St. Barbara and the two winged genii (visible at the bottom of the picture space) symbolize the funeral ceremony. The canvas was located in the Convent of St. Sixtus in Piacenza and was later donated by the monks to Augustus III, King of Saxony. It was carried to Moscow after the Second World War, and was later returned to Dresden. The Virgin appears actually to descend from a heavenly space, through the picture plane, out into the real space in which the painting is hung. The gesture of St. Sixtus and the glance of St. Barbara seem to be directed toward the faithful, whom we imagine beyond the ballustrade at the bottom of the painting. The Papal tiara, which rests on top of this ballustrade, acts as a bridge between the real and pictorial space. Here again, the work incorporates a portrait of Julius II, this time as Pope Sixtus. The portrait, in Vasari's words, is "so lively and truthful that ... it seems alive." The original painting was intended for the church of Santa Maria del Popolo in Rome, but never arrived there. The Uffizi canvas is a copy which arrived in the Medici collections in Florence from Urbino with the Della Rovere inheritance. Attributed by critics to 1512, it shows the Pope seated with the tiara on his head, dressed in a white surplice and a purple mantle. Here the simple but effective tonal contrast which was first used in the *Portrait of a Cardinal* reappears. The Pope, though old, still seems very vigorous and the Della Rovere energy is clearly visible in the hand that grasps the right arm of the chair with strength and pride. The two acorn-shaped knobs on the back of the chair recall the Pope's coat of arms. The intimacy of the image, although weakened by the executor of the copy, indicates that Raphael has progressed from the narrative compositions of the Vatican Stanze to the full dominance of individual subjectivity.

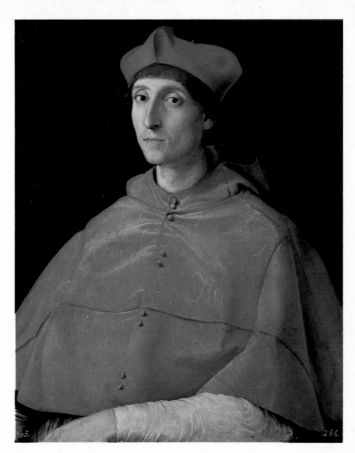

Above: Portrait of a Cardinal. Madrid, Prado.
Various attempts have been made to identify the subject of this portrait. The painting, dated 1510-11, is one of Raphael's more successful portraits. It is principally known for its chromatic and psychological content.

Opposite page, above: Leo the Great and Attila (Stanza di Eliodoro).
The episode shows the meeting between Pope Leo the Great and Attila the Hun near Rome in which, according to tradition, the Pope evoked the armed figures of Saints Peter and Paul in order to block the barbarian invasion of the Papal city. Much of the painting was executed by Raphael's followers.

Opposite page, below: The Fire in the Borgo (Stanza dell'incendio di Borgo).
This room is named after the painting reproduced here. The painting represents the fire which swept through the Roman quarter near St. Peter's (the Borgo) and which was extinguished by the intercession of Pope Leo IV. The other scenes of the cycle, which was executed between 1514 and 1517, were painted by Raphael's followers, particularly Giulio Romano. The protagonists of the scenes are all popes named Leo. The room celebrates the greatness of Pope Leo X, Julius II's successor.

ΑΝΝΗ ΠΑΡΘΕΝΟΤΟΚΩ
ΠΑΡΘΕΝΙΚΗ ΘΕΟΤΟΚΩ
Κ ΛΥΤΡΩΤΗ ΧΡΙΣΤΩ
·ΙΩ· ΚΟΡ·

The Prophet Isaiah. Rome, Sant'Agostino.
The fresco is usually dated 1511-12. It was painted
for Giovanni Goritz of Luxemburg, Head Chancellor
of the Papal Court. The Greek and Hebrew inscriptions
underline the religious character of the work.
The energetic figure clearly shows
the influence of Michelangelo.

Opposite page: Galatea. Rome, Farnesina.
Raphael painted the Galatea in 1512
for the Roman villa of the Sienese banker, Agostino Chigi.
The painting is inspired by a classical poem. It shows
the nymph, Galatea, amid a train of water gods and amorini.

Meanwhile, Raphael had also passed from the highly synthetic and expressive compositions of the first years of the decade to representations which were more and more complex and even more dispersive. Most of these were finished by his pupils as well, for, as we mentioned above, this was the busiest moment in Raphael's career.

The *Madonna dell'Impannata* in the Palatine Gallery in Florence was also painted with the help of assistants. According to some critics, the assistants executed the entire painting. But others see the master's hand at least in the major figures (some say in the Christ child, some in St. Elizabeth, some in both figures). The composition is innovative in respect to the usual iconography of the holy family. It shows St. Catherine, St. Elizabeth, Christ, the Virgin and St. John gathered together in a group. A large tent is visible in the background and a window covered by linen (the "impannato" or curtain which gives the painting its name) can be seen at the extreme right. Like many other works by Raphael, this painting was carried off by the French in 1799 and was not returned until after the Congress of Vienna, in 1815.

In 1514 Raphael executed another small but significant fresco cycle for Agostino Chigi. The frescoes represent the *Prophets and Sibyls*. They are located in the chapel at the left of the apse of the church of Santa Maria della Pace in Rome. The figures occupy a trabeated loggia, on two levels. The structure of the loggia reflects the architecture of the chapel: its arches coincide with those of the window and entrance. The *Prophets* (Habakkuk, Jonah, David and Daniel, according to the most widely accepted interpretation) are generally attributed to a collaborator (perhaps Timoteo Viti) who must have based them on an original drawing by Raphael, for they are highly coherent. The *Sibyls* (Cumaean, Persian, Phrygian and Tiburtine) are attributed to Raphael. Like the Virtues in the Stanza della Segnatura, each of the figures is accompanied by an angel who indicates the divine spirit present in their prophecies. Between the Sibyls at the top of the arch is a small angel holding a lighted torch, the symbol of prophesy, which enlightens the darkness of the future.

Raphael followed Leo X when he went to Bologna to meet the King of France, Francis I, in 1515. He may have passed through Florence, where Leo was welcomed with great enthusiasm by his fellow citizens. Leonardo da Vinci—who later accepted the French King's invitation to Paris—and Michelangelo—to whom Leo X commissioned the New Sacresty of San Lorenzo—also followed the Pope.

A letter which Raphael sent to the painter, Francesco Francia, provides proof of this journey. According to a legend, Francesco Francia died after seeing the *Saint Cecilia* which Raphael painted for the church of San Giovanni in Monte in Bologna. The story is almost credible, for the Bolognese artistic environment still revolved around the style of Perugino. The painting, which is presently in the Museum of Bologna, was placed in San Giovanni in Monte in 1515. It was painted some time before, however. The figures represent St. Paul, St. John the Evangelist, St. Cecilia, St. Augustine and St. Mary Magdalen. The four saints who surround the protagonist form a niche which is strengthened by the poses and gestures of the figures (the glances of the Evangelist and St. Augustine cross, St. Paul's is lowered and the Magdalen turns hers toward the spectator). Only St. Cecilia

Right: Madonna del Duca D'Alba.
Washington, National Gallery.
This tondo is dated 1511.
It shows the indirect influence
of Michelangelo.

Opposite page, above:
Galatea (detail).
The torsion in the character's limbs
derives from Michelangelo, but
the formal beauty and composite
quality of the figures
are peculiar to Raphael.

Opposite page, below: Palemone
(detail of the Galatea).
The young Palemone, holding
the reins of a dolphin, drives
Galatea's triumphal chariot.

raises her face toward the sky, where a chorus of angels appears through a hole in the clouds. The monumentality of the figures, typical of Raphael's activity during this period, dominates the other figurative elements. The still life of musical instruments on the ground has been attributed to Raphael's pupil Giovanni da Udine, according to a tradition begun by Vasari.

The *Madonna della Sedia* in the Pitti Gallery in Florence, was probably painted during the period immediately after the completion of the Stanza di Eliodoro. The coloristic and luministic qualities which this tondo possesses result in great compositional harmony. A circular motif dominates the painting, in perfect agreement with the form of the support. The Virgin is by no means conceived in aristocratic terms. Her clothes are modest, and even the maternal sentiment expressed in the painting is not altered by the knowledge of its sacred nature. Rather, it is expressed in an instinctive gesture of affectionate protection of the Child. The rich and polished back of the chair which gives the work its name (*sedia* means chair) thus stands in clear contrast to the figure. The young St. John fills the space left free by the group of the Virgin and Child and balances the composition, though remaining outside the affective relationship which links mother and Child.

Many critics associate the composition of the *Madonna della Sedia* with that of the *Madonna della Tenda* (so called because of the curtain which forms the background) in the Altepinakothek of Munich. Here again the Madonna is shown in a three-quarters view with the Child and the young St. John. But a relationship exists among the figures which was absent in the *Madonna*

della Sedia. The Virgin smiles at her Child, whose attention is turned toward St. John. The face of the latter bears an expression of affectionate devotion. By comparing Raphael's mature works to one another, one detects a process of continuous growth, of stylistic evolution. The elements used are always new, as is the pictorial style. But the master's extraordinary capacity to harmonize the composition and the formal beauty of the figures, made more evident by the expression of serene emotion, are unifying motifs.

There are two extant versions of Raphael's portrait of *Cardinal Inghirami*: one in Boston and the other in Palazzo Pitti. Each has been considered the original at one time or another, but the dispute is useless, since both are highly coherent and the differences between them are small: the physical structure of the Cardinal is more massive in the Boston portrait and leaner in the Pitti one. The red of the Cardinal's clothing dominates both. Inghirami's crossed eyes, a physical defect which the artist does not avoid, acquire a discreet tone which almost dissolves in the inspired pose of the figure. Without idealizing, but also without falling into unpleasant naturalism, Raphael maintains a harmonic equilibrium between realism and dignified celebration, a primary characteristic of portrait painting.

The *Portrait of Baldassarre Castiglione* (now in the Louvre), a literary figure active at the court of Urbino in the first years of the 15th century and author of the *Courtesan*, the book which summed up the tastes and culture of the Renaissance, may or may not have been painted by Raphael. According to a letter of 1516 from Pietro Bembo to Cardinal Bibbiena, "The portrait of M.

Baldassarre Castiglione... [and that of Duke Guidobaldo di Montefeltro] would seem to be by the hand of one of Raphael's pupils." But the high quality and masterful combination of pictorial elements which distinguish the painting (note the affection inherent in the intelligent and calm face of Castiglione) lead one to think that the master participated in some way in its execution. Certainly the shaded tonalities of the clothing and the unusually light background indicate the hand of a skillful and experienced painter.

Also in 1516, Agostino Chigi commissioned the decoration of his chapel in Santa Maria del Popolo to Raphael. Raphael designed the architecture of the chapel and planned Agostino's tomb. He prepared the cartoons for the mosaic of the dome, fusing together classical motives (the Planets, represented as pagan gods) and Christian ones (the figure of God the Father who sets the heavens in motion with an authoritative gesture). But his activity in this year included other works as well. He was widely recognized at the humanistic court of Leo X, who made him the architect of St. Peter's on August 1, 1514, and this increased his work load. He was placed in charge of the marble which came to St. Peter's from excavations and from antique monuments. He gathered statues, medals and antique objects for Alfonso I d'Este. Finally, he tried his hand as a sculptor. The largest task he undertook in the course of the year

Left: The Sistine Madonna. Dresda, Gemäldegalerie. This painting, possibly executed for the tomb of Julius II, comes from the church of San Sisti in Piacenza. It is one of the rare works of Raphael executed on canvas. It is dated 1513-14.

Right: The Madonna di Foligno. Rome, Vatican Museum. Sigismondo de' Conti commissioned this painting to Raphael as a votive offering to commemorate the salvation of his house from fire. The painting is dated 1511-12. The figure of the Virgin and the atmospheric effects of the background are particularly beautiful.

Opposite page: Landscape (detail of the Madonna di Foligno). A thunderbolt strikes the Conti house from the clouds above, creating subtle lighting effects throughout the surrounding landscape.

was the preparation of the cartoons for the tapestries for the Sistine Chapel, which contained the *Stories of Saints Peter and Paul*. The completed tapestries were acquired by Charles I, King of England, and are now in the Victoria and Albert Museum in London.

The *Donna Velata* in Palazzo Pitti is another portrait dated 1516. Tradition identifies the subject with "la Fornarina," the woman whom the painter loved in his last years and whose face reappeared in his paintings and in those of his followers. The painting shows greater attention to color and to the rendering of skin and clothes in respect to previous female portraits. The regular oval of the young woman's face stands out against the dark background and her eyes hold an intense and penetrating look. The silk of her sleeves contrasts with her ivory-like skin, and is closely associated with the thin pleating of the dress, held up by a corset with golden embroidery. As in the portrait of Castiglione, the figure radiates a sense of great dignity and restraint. But greys and light blues dominated the portrait of Castiglione: here the warm tonalities of white and gold take over. Raphael is preparing the wider color range and the more complex composition which will be expressed in the portrait of Leo X.

During this period Raphael was sought by priests and cardinals who competed in the decoration of their mansions in Rome. Cardinal Bernardo Dovizi da Bibbiena, a cultured playwright, and (like Leo X) a passionate scholar of classical antiquity, undoubtedly had more contact with Raphael than any of his colleagues. Raphael painted a *Portrait* of the Cardinal which clearly expressed his shrewd and malicious spirit and his taste for beautiful things and fine living. The attribution of the portrait (now in the Pitti Gallery) is not certain, but the composition and the

Left: Portrait of Pope Julius II. Florence, Uffizi.
This painting may be a replica of an original executed by Raphael for the church of Santa Maria del Popolo, in Rome. It arrived in Florence with the patrimony of the Della Rovere family.

Right: Portrait of Cardinal Fedra Inghirami.
Florence, Palazzo Pitti.
Raphael painted two versions of this portrait (the other is in the Isabella Stewart Gardner Museum in Boston), at different times.
The Pitti portrait is dated 1512-15.

Left: Portrait of Baldassarre Castiglione.
Paris, Louvre.
A refined sense of color based on grey and blue tones
characterizes this portrait of the humanist writer
and friend of Raphael. The portrait is dated 1514-15.

Right: Portrait of Cardinal Bibbiena.
Florence, Palazzo Pitti.
This painting is probably a contemporary copy
of an original by Raphael. It represents the lively
and cultured personality of Bernardo Dovizi da Bibbiena,
playwright, literary figure, and Raphael's
patron at the Papal court.

characteristic use of white and red suggest Raphael's hand. However, the rendering seems more rigid than that in the paintings certainly painted by Raphael. Some critics therefore attribute it to a pupil of Raphael, or suspect that it may be a copy of an original which might have been lost. The cardinal was so familiar with the artist that he offered his neice, Marietta, in marriage.

In the same year as the *Portrait* (1516), Raphael and his followers were commissioned to decorate the bathroom of the Cardinal's Vatican apartments, the so-called *Stufetta.* The ornamental motives employed in the *Stufetta* paintings derive from those of the *Domus Aurea*, the villa of the Emperor Nero between the Palatine Hill and the Velia. The *Domus Aurea* had recently been rediscovered. By 1516 it had become an object of great enthusiasm for contemporary artists. The names of Giovanni da Udine, Domenichino and other lesser known painters are still visible, scratched in the walls of the monument. Raphael painted the *Story of Venus* on the walls of the *Stufetta*, perhaps at the suggestion of the Cardinal. He represented the episodes of the story in the same techniques used in the *Domus Aurea*: stucco and fresco. The decoration of the borders started a new ornamental style, called "grotesque," which derives from the decoration of the "grotto" of Nero's villa. The new style was widely used throughout the Cinquecento and after. It replaced the "candelabro" motif of the Quattrocento, which was generally made up of plants, animals and stylized putti growing out of a vase or amphora. Raphael thus left his mark in the field of decorative tastes as well as in that of pictorial style.

In the following year, 1517, Agostino Chigi commissioned Raphael to decorate the ground floor loggia of the villa in which he had painted the *Galatea* five years before. Like the *Galatea* and the *Stufetta*, this cycle reflects the cultured atmosphere which flourished in Rome under Julius II and Leo X. The frescos represent the *Story of Psyche*, a myth derived from the *Golden Ass* of Apuleius (II century A. D.). Although the preparatory drawings and the general conception of the stories are by Raphael, the bulk of the painting was carried out by his pupils, notably Giovanni da Udine (who painted the rich plant festoons of the frame) with the collaboration of Giulio Romano, Raphaelino del Colle and Gianfrancesco Penni. The two major scenes were painted in the vault. They are *The Marriage of Cupid and Psiche* and the *Council of the Gods*, conceived in terms of tapestries and embroideries.

Some elements deriving from Michelangelo are present in Raphael's works from the period after 1517. *The Vision of Ezekiel* is a typical example. The *Vision* shows the same balanced composition present throughout Raphael's works. The origin of the subject is the Bible (*Ezekiel*, 1: 4-12). But instead of describing the four *Kerubim* (inspired by Babylonian iconography) as the Prophet did, Raphael represents a classical divinity with the traditional

symbols of the Evangelists. Vasari describes the painting as "a Christ, as Jupiter, floating in the sky, surrounded by the four Evangelists." A centrally placed tree dominates the low, broad landscape and the sky is turbulent and stormy. The divine group hovers amid the clouds, surrounded by an aura of bright light. The angel, eagle, lion and ox which symbolize the Evangelists, together with two cherubs, spiral around the vigorous central figure. The painting, now in the Pitti Gallery in Florence, is believed to have been painted in 1518. Like many other paintings by Raphael, it was removed to Paris by Napoleon's army and returned to Tuscany in 1815.

Raphael was very active during the last two years of his life. Francis I, King of France, commissioned two paintings to him in 1518: the first representing *St. Michael* and the second, the *Holy Family*. Critics have attributed both to Raphael's workshop, underlining the chairoscuro effects and the leaden tones which mark them. Raphael himself was engaged with his project for the decoration of the Vatican Logge, which were completed in 1519.

But his greatest masterpiece, possibly the only work which he executed without help during these last years,

St. Cecilia.
Bologna, Pinacoteca Nazionale.
This panel was executed in 1514
for the convent of San Giovanni
in Monte, in Bologna. The innovative
structure of the composition (whose
traditional 'sacra conversazione' format
includes the onlookers but not
the object of their devotion)
and the unusual 'still life' of objects
in the foreground make this work
one of Raphael's
more original creations.

Opposite page:
The Madonna della Seggiola.
Florence, Palazzo Pitti.
This panel is usually dated 1514.
Warm, luminous tones enrich
the extremely simple composition.

is the *Portrait of Pope Leo X and Cardinals Luigi de'
Rossi and Giulio de' Medici* (later to become Pope Clement
VII), both relatives of the Pope. This group portrait
(which created a sensation, notwithstanding the existence
of precedents) is focused on the central figure of the Pope.
The two Cardinals, Luigi de' Rossi on Leo's right (whose
sharp features, modelled by strong chiaroscuro effects,
suggest the hand of Giulio Romano) and Giulio de' Medici on his left, act as a royal escort. An illuminated
prayer book is opened on the table in front of Pope Leo.
On the same table rests a finely carved bell. Both objects
undoubtedly reveal the exquisite tastes of the Pope who
was, as we have seen, an active patron of the arts. The

uniform tone of color, expressed in various red nuances; the
quiet atmosphere, allusive to the power of the Pope and
the splendor of his court; and the compositional harmony
make this portrait one of the more admired and significant
works of Raphael. These paintings symbolically close the
painter's career. He had enjoyed the patronage of two
Popes and his presence in Rome had made the city the
most important artistic center in Italy.

His Map of ancient Rome was dedicated to this task and
to recovering evidence of Rome's former greatness. He
worked on it throughout 1519, and aroused great enthusiasm. A letter of praise, written in Latin after the death of
the artist by Castiglione, summarizes this enthusiasm.

Much of Raphael's energy during these last years was directed toward public activity, or at least toward commissioners who were influential in city life and life within the Papal States (he designed a villa, known as the *Villa Madama*, for Cardinal Giulio de' Medici). Furthermore, many critics attribute to him a series of compositions of the *Holy Family* and of *Saints* which were generally executed by his followers. The famous portrait of a young woman, called *La Fornarina*, must also be viewed in this perspective, although it is signed, in Latin, "Raphael from Urbino." The signature is engraved on the thin ribbon that the girl wears just under her left shoulder. Tradition identifies her with Margherita Luti, a Sienese woman whom Raphael loved, the daughter of a banker from the Roman district of Santa Dorotea. The stiffness of her features and the heavy chairoscuro effect make *La Fornarina* an almost certain workshop piece, for Raphael's own work from this period is far more delicate.

According to Vasari, Raphael's pupils—among them Giulio Romano, Gianfrancesco Penni, Vincenzo Tamagni, Perin del Vaga and Polidoro da Caravaggio—executed a cycle of thirteen *Bible Stories* in the vaults of the Logge adjoining the buildings that Bramante had built in the Vatican for Julius II. The Gallery was planned by Raphael, who also projected a decorative cycle of grotesques and stucco-reliefs. The latter were executed according to the

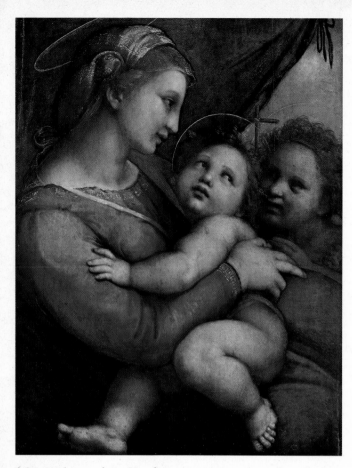

The Madonna della Tenda.
Munich, Alte Pinakothek.
The composition of this painting is similar to that
of the Madonna della Seggiola, but is characterized
by a more synthethic treatment
of the details. The painting is dated 1514.

Opposite page: The Donna Velata.
Florence, Palazzo Pitti.
This painting is dated 1516. Tradition identifies
the subject with Margherita Luti (better known
as 'la Fornarina'), the woman whom Raphael
loved during his last years in Rome.

ancient technique studied during the excavation of the *Domus Aurea*. The *Bible Stories* occupied Raphael's workshop from 1518 to 1519. They are known both for their inherent pictorial value and for the influence they had on later decorative cycles.

The Biblical episodes were painted in the ceiling vaults, within differently shaped frames. Together they form a swarm of figures, isolated and in groups, arranged in an extraordinary variety of compositions and poses. Michelangelo's *Doni Tondo* introduced mannerism as a principle of figure design; the Vatican *Logge* introduced descriptive mannerism, a style of painting divorced from the precepts and principles of the early Renaissance. This style gave rise to lively and refined images packed with allusions, symbols and allegories, and often inspired by literary texts. It soon became an international movement. It was used with, or instead of, the classicizing tendency from which it was born, throughout the 16th century.

Raphael's pupils later reaffirmed their interest in classical antiquity and its interpretation in the decoration of the *Loggetta*, a small porch adjacent to the above mentioned *Bath* of Cardinal Bibbiena. The decorative program consisted of grotesque figures and of scenes from the Apollo myth. Only two of the three original paintings have been preserved. The scholar, Redig de Campos, reconstructed the third scene, whose theme was almost certainly the Flaying of Marsyas. The other two scenes represent Olympus praying to Apollo, and Apollo and Marsyas. Architectural structures, animals, winged cherubs and false niches containing reproductions of statues (which Redig de Campos has identified as the *Seasons*)—similar to those which appear in Roman wall paintings—accompany the three scenes. This refined decorative complex was the logical completion of the *Logge* and the last reflection of the classical tendencies of art at the court of Leo X. Raphael was overwhelmed by commissions by this time. He dedicated himself to the design and planning of the works which were entrusted to him, and left the material execution to his pupils. The latter participated (together with Sebastiano del Piombo, who painted in a Michelangelo-like style) in the decoration of the fourth room of the Vatican Palace, the Stanza di Costantino. Here Raphael's influence is weaker than in other works. The figures are extremely agitated. They violate that norm which Raphael observed even in his more dynamic creations, for instance, the frescoes for the Stanza di Eliodoro.

Raphael's health deteriorated rapidly, undermined by his relentless activity and by the excesses of his private life. It prevented him from finishing the *Transfiguration* now in the Vatican Museum. Vasari, not without prejudice, compares the unrestrained life of Raphael to the austere and heroic one of Michelangelo, of whom he was a passionate admirer and around whose art he had structured his *Lives of the Artists*. Cardinal Giulio de' Medici commissioned the *Transfiguration* to Raphael for the French Cathedral of Narbonne.

The composition of the *Transfiguration* is divided into two distinct parts: the Miracle of the Possessed Boy on a lower level, in the foreground; and the Transfiguration of Christ on Mt. Tabor, in the background. The transfigured Christ floats in an aura of light and clouds above the hill, accompanied by Moses and Elijah. Below, on the ground, are his disciples. Some are dazzled by the light

The Vision of Ezekiel.
Florence, Palazzo Pitti.
Raphael interprets the Biblical story
in an exceptionally energetic
composition featuring God the Father
surrounded by the symbols
of the Evangelists.
The work is usually dated 1518.

Opposite page: The Loggia of Psyche.
Rome, The Farnesina.
Raphael conceived this rich and
balanced composition in 1517 for
Agostino Chigi, as a decoration
for the porch of his Roman villa.
It depicts the Legend of Psyche,
as it appears in The Golden Ass
of Apuleius. Raphael's pupils
participated extensively
in the execution of the fresco.

of glory, others are in prayer. The gestures of the crowd present at the miracle link the two parts together: the raised hands of the crowd converge toward the figure of Christ. According to tradition, the painting was completed by Raphael's followers after his death. Giulio Romano, Raphael's heir, was paid for the work. Extant documents suggest, however, that Raphael delegated the work to his pupils while he was still alive. The *Transfiguration* is the last bequest of an artist whose brief life was rich in

inspiration, where doubt or tension had no place. Raphael's life was spent in thoughts of great harmony and balance. This is one of the reasons why Raphael appears as the best interpreter of the art of his time and has been admired and studied in every century.

On April 6, 1520, precisely 37 years after he was born, Raphael died in Rome, the city that he had helped make the most important center of art and culture that had ever existed.

Opposite page: The 'Stufetta'. Rome, Vatican.
Raphael decorated the bath of Cardinal Dovizi
di Bibbiena's Vatican apartments in 1516
with the help of collaborators.
It is painted in a style which recalls classical Roman
mural decoration.

Above, left: The 'Logge'. Rome, Vatican.
The decoration of the thirteen vaults of the portico
of the Vatican Palace was a major undertaking
for the school of Raphael.
The stucco and fresco paintings, executed in 1518-19,
represent scenes from the Old and New Testaments.
The ornamental motifs are inspired by those
of classical mural painting.

Above, right: The 'Loggetta'. Rome, Vatican.
Raphael's workshop executed the 'grotesque'
decoration of this small porch adjacent
to Cardinal Bibbiena's bath, in 1519.
The paintings represent Apollo and Marsyas
and the Four Seasons.

Below: The 'Loggetta' (details).
These ornamental motifs derive from classical mural painting.
They indicate the strict 'archaeological' attention
directed toward antique art in Raphael's time.

Opposite page: La Fornarina. Rome, National Gallery.   *Cartoons for the Vatican Tapestries.*
London, Victoria and Albert Museum.

71

*Portrait of Pope Leo X with Cardinals Luigi de' Rossi
and Giulio de' Medici. Florence, Uffizi.*

The Transfiguration

by Fabrizio Mancinelli

The *Transfiguration* hung peacefully in the church of San Pietro in Montorio on the Janiculum until 1797, when Napoleon took it and other masterpieces to Paris. Not all the works arrived in Paris in good condition and many (the *Madonna of Foligno* and the *Coronation of the Virgin*, for example) had to be restored. The color layer of these paintings was removed from the original support and transferred to a new one. The Louvre technicians proposed the same solution for the *Transfiguration*, but fortunately the process was never carried out (the painting may have been too large to permit the transfer). A metal framework was added to reinforce the old wooden support. But this structure, instead of conserving the painting, caused new damages: cracks in the wooden support were not permitted to expand freely. As a consequence, previous damage was worsened and new injuries developed.

The most extensive operation the French performed was to clean and varnish the painting. The cleaning was necessary, for the painting was extremely dirty and the original varnish had darkened with time, making it practically impossible to see the painting. The process was executed with the means available at the time, and, unfortunately, it caused some damage. This damage is most visible in the head of St. Andrew (the father of the young boy) and in certain zones of the sky, but it extends to the rest of the picture surface as well. The varnishing brought more serious consequences. The varnish was not neutral, but was treated with Avignon yellow. This pigment radically modified the general tonality of the painting, in which cold tones originally prevailed. It also flattened the composition, for the yellow pigment was stronger on the light colors and weaker on the dark ones. Expedients of this type were frequently used throughout the 19th century and during the first years of the 20th. They were partially determined by contemporary tastes, which imposed their deforming esthetic on the painting. The varnish deteriorated with time, completely changing the painting's color range (before the recent restoration the predominant tones were green rather than blue).

Numerous problems faced the technicians who carried out the restoration of 1972-1976. The operation was executed in the Painting Laboratory of the Vatican Museums under the supervision of Dr. D. Redig de Campos and myself. The restorers were L. Brandi, E. Guidi and M. Mattarocci, who collaborated with Dr. N. Gabrielli of the Museums' Scientific Laboratory and with technicians F. Dati, G. Barnia and G. Morresi. The problem of the support was solved by removing the French framework and applying a new flexible wooden framework to the panel (whose defects had been corrected). The new framework allows the wood to expand and contract freely but prevents it from warping. The panel is now supported by a specially designed metal structure which also sustains the individual elements of the wooden framework.

Cleaning the painting did not present great difficulties: the main problem was to remove the yellow pigment, the bad varnish and the old stucco which in many places covered the original colors. The latter were still intact.

The painting has been restored to its original state, which can be deduced from an 18th century mosaic in St. Peter's. The restoration has permitted critics to make several interesting discoveries. The first and most visible of these concerns color. The original color of the painting is essentially cold. Its nuances are subtle and accurate, with extremely refined effects of irridescent, porcelain-like tones. It is a 'Venetian' color determined by, and expressed through, the light. It accentuates the actions of the figures. Raphael used these tones to underline the symbolic and compositional unity of the painting, which draws together two distinct episodes (the Transfiguration and the Miracle of the Possessed Boy).

The composition is divided into two zones which correspond to the two parts of the narrative. The figures are enclosed by two circles which converge toward a common point much like an open oyster shell, whose two halves converge at the hinge. The upper level contains the principle event, in which the two Prophets rotate in space around the central figure of Christ. X-ray analyses have shown that Raphael sketched the figures of Christ, the Prophets and Saint John nude in order to balance their movements in space.

The Miracle of the Possessed Boy takes place in the lower zone. It is a moment of anxiety, doubt and impotence. It counterbalances the transcendental light emanating from the image of Christ, a visual device designed to attract the attention of the spectator, who is drawn into the action by the gestures of the excited figures in the crowd, each of which clearly expresses a characteristic emotional reaction. The two scenes are bound together by the light, which emphasizes the gestures on the one hand — with effects, in the lower part, of an exasperated *luminismo* which must have appealed to Caravaggio several decades later and which may have originated in Raphael's theatrical experience of these years — and underlines the transcendental nature of the miracle on the other. The light plunges both scenes into a wide range of cold tonalities which is meaningfully balanced by the warm light of the sunset over the landscape background.

The restoration also revealed that the work was left by Raphael as we see it now. That Raphael might have left it incomplete was suggested by payments made to Giulio Romano after Raphael's death. But the payments can be explained by the fact that Giulio Romano was Raphael's heir, and Raphael died before collecting the whole sum that was due him. In any case, the painting is complete except for some final tuoches. That these final touches have been left uncompleted rules out the possibility that the *Transfiguration* was finished by Raphael's workshop after his death (only the final varnishing can be attributed to the workshop).

The most notable unfinished elements are in the lower half of the picture. In the extreme foreground, a brown rock is merely sketched in and the grass that covers it lacks the luministic accents that play over the rest of the grass. The hands of the boy's father are also sketched in; the right one shows a change in the original position. The robe of the figure behind the father, at the extreme right of the picture, is also incomplete. The same is true for the arm of the most distant foreground figure, who points at the miracle of the Transfiguration. The right foot of the Prophet Elijah is unfinished and Christ's right hand (unlike his left) is flat and lacks the final glazing. The two deacons at the left are also very probably unfinished. There are probably other parts of the painting which Raphael was unable to complete, but the delicate condition of the painting prevents a more thorough cleaning and a more precise analysis.

The presence of these unfinished parts throws new light on the problem of workshop participation and the authorship of the painting. There is no doubt that his pupils cooperated with Raphael in executing the painting, for many of the preparatory drawings can be attributed to Penni and Giulio Romano. But critics had asserted in the past that Raphael's helpers had also executed whole figures and figure groups (particularly the group of the possessed child and his relatives). Now — in addition to the great coherence of some of the controversial figures (namely those of the Possessed Boy and the woman kneeling in the foreground), which the recent cleaning fully revealed — the restoration and the X-ray examination which preceded it have produced new evidence which should end the dispute.

Many changes were made between the original conception of the *Transfiguration* and the painting as it appears today. Some of these are visible to the naked eye and others have been revealed by X-rays. Many are small and simple (the change in position of Christ's feet or of the woman kneeling in the foreground). Others are more substantial. The latter can be found in three figures only: the so-called St. Andrew, the kneeling woman and the

The Transfiguration (before restoration).
Rome, Vatican Museum.
The sources indicate that Cardinal Giulio de' Medici commissioned the Transfiguration to Raphael in 1517.

Opposite page: The Transfiguration (after restoration).

74

*Opposite page; above: The Father of the Possessed Boy
after restoration and in X-ray.
Below: The Possessed Boy before and after restoration.*

*Christ with Apostles and Prophets
(detail, after restoration).*

father of the child. The latter two are the most significant, for they involve controversial figures. In both cases the more substantial changes concern the heads. The father was bald in the drawings, with flowing black hair. The arch of his brow was lower. The eyebrows themselves were knitted in a skeptical expression which mixed with discouragement, evident in the curve of his lips. In the final version of the painting his head is covered with thick hair held in place by a headband. His brow is less arched and his features, less tense. His face as a whole is a mask of crystallized emotion. The same transformation took place in the face of the kneeling woman. In the preliminary sketch her hair is less elaborately arranged. It is held in place by a large band which covers the top of her head. Strands of hair fall onto her forehead, breaking up her pure profile. In the final versions the profile is unbroken: it continues up to the line of her finely curled hair. The change is important, for it eliminates the naturalistic touch which characterized the face in the preliminary drawing, transforming it into an idealized mask, an abstract symbol of classical beauty.

These changes show the long and involved process of working and reworking the figures which underlies the painting. It also reveals a body of precise stylistic research that is difficult to attribute to the workshop and can be explained only by the direct involvement of Raphael. Less coherent passages occur here and there, but they can be ascribed to the cleaning done during the 19th century restoration in those cases in which these parts were not left unfinished by the artist. Careful analysis shows that the *Transfiguration* represents the masterful realization of the artists' ideas.

In 1514 Raphael wrote a letter to Castiglione in which he said, "In order to paint a beautiful woman I must see women who are more beautiful, and you must help me to find the best. But since there is a lack of good judges and beautiful women, I follow a certain Idea that is in my mind." All the figures represented in the painting have prototypes which can be found in the past experiences of the artist, in the work of such contemporaries as Leonardo or in classical antiquity. The head of St. Andrew in the first sketch, for instance, derives from the preparatory drawing for the portrait of Bramante in the *Disputà*. This figure, who looks with a brooding face over the shoulder of his neighbor, is a citation from the Uffizi *Adoration of the Magi* by Leonardo. Finally, the head of the father in the preparatory drawing probably derives from that of the Scyta (also in the Uffizi) who prepares to flay Marsyas.

A sketch-book probably existed for the use of the workshop, but in the painting the models seem to have been reworked in a search for transcendent perfection and purified of every excessive emotion. Furthermore, some figures are based on more than one model: for example, the head of St. Andrew, at least in the drawing for it, is derived from the so-called Bramante of the *Disputa*, while the body is derived from the Horace of the *Parnassus*, seen in reverse.

From what we have said the fame of the *Transfiguration* — both among Raphael's contemporaries and after his death — appears fully justified today. Beside the direct influence it had on the mannerists, the painting presents elements which anticipate later artistic developments. The interpretation of the landscape, for instance, foreshadows that of the second half of the 16th century and of the Carracci. The use of light, which defines the outline of the figures, isolating them through their gestures, anticipates the art of the 17th century, including that of Caravaggio.

Above: The Meadow (detail, after restoration).
The rock to the right is only roughly sketched.

Below: The so-called St. Andrew (detail, after restoration).

Opposite page: Landscape (detail, after restoration).
The second hand is unfinished.

Contents

List of Illustrations